WHITE HOUSE PHYSICIAN

WHITE HOUSE PHYSICIAN

By Vice-Admiral Ross T. McIntire

SURGEON GENERAL OF THE NAVY

In Collaboration with

GEORGE CREEL

G. P. PUTNAM'S SONS

NEW YORK

Copyright, 1946, by Ross T. McIntire and George Creel

Manufactured in the United States of America

VAN REES PRESS · NEW YORK

Contents

CONTENTS

WHITE HOUSE PHYSICIAN

CHAPTER I

MY REASON FOR WRITING

FROM THE DAY OF HIS FIRST INAUGURATION IN 1933 until the moment of his passing, I had the privilege of close and continuous companionship with Franklin D. Roosevelt in my capacity as White House physician. I saw him each morning and again in the evening, for the care of the President of the United States cannot be haphazard but necessitates constant watch. I went with him on his many journeys both at home and abroad, and the co-operation of a devoted secretariat kept me informed as to what went on when he was not under my eye. Marguerite Le Hand, Marvin McIntyre, Grace Tully, "Pa" Watson, and Steve Early were as much members of my staff as though they held medical degrees. Here, then, was no casual association, but one marked for more than twelve years by the intimacy so inseparable from the relationship between doctor and patient.

Throughout this long stretch the thing that amazed me most, and still amazes, was that not one of the thousands who conferred with him ever regarded the

3

President as a *cripple*. Nor did any of the millions who saw him and listened to him, as he campaigned or made the coast-to-coast tours of the country that were his keenest pleasure. As he sat, only his mighty wrestler's torso showing above the desk or table, he exhaled fitness and well-being, and even when he stood, balanced by steel braces that were plainly evident, the single impression was strength and abounding vitality.

Just as the President had schooled himself to ignore his infirmity, so did he bring everybody about him to the same unawareness. The click of his braces as he got up and down, and the wheel chair itself, soon failed to register. On many trips, where his eager interest insisted on seeing some place that could not be reached by car or boat, we made a cradle of our hands and carried him, but even then it never occurred to any of us to think of him as helpless.

I remember particularly an occasion at the White House during the time that Mme Chiang Kai-shek was a guest, having come from China to beg larger aid for her invaded homeland. On leaving the room at the end of the evening, she turned to the President with a flutter of her graceful hands and told him not to go to the bother of getting up. Only when he pointed to his braces did Mme Chiang realize what she had said, and while a wave of color flushed her face, the President laughed and thanked her for the compliment.

This was not an isolated incident, but quite common. I was with him at the Atlantic Charter meeting,

4

Casablanca, Teheran, Cairo, Malta, and Yalta, and
watched carefully the reactions of the Allied leaders
that he was meeting for the first time. Stalin, Chiang
Kai-shek, King Farouk, General de Gaulle, ibn-Saud,
Haile Selassie, and all the others had a moment of
natural curiosity about the President's physical condition, but inside of an hour his sheer virility had its
usual effect.

This was what Franklin Roosevelt himself, serenely
and indomitably, had *willed*. As a usual thing, he
avoided all allusion to that black morning in Campobello when he awakened to find that his aching,
paralyzed legs would not lift his body from the bed.
No man was ever more resolute in facing forward.
Once, however, as we sat alone, some turn of the conversation unlocked his lips. It was a bad time, he
confessed, when the doctors told him that it was not
rheumatism, muscular strain, or anything else that
would soon pass, but infantile paralysis. All the horror
of a lifetime of helplessness swept over him, for poliomyelitis was then a mysterious disease for which there
seemed to be no cure.

There was terror in that first rush of anguish, but
catching hold of himself, he gritted his teeth and resolved to "lick it." Never, never, never would he accept
invalidism as a rule of life, sitting on the side lines and
living by proxy. If resolution and determination had
anything to do with it, he *would* walk again. Failing
that, he would so crowd his days with interests and

5

activities that the thought of infirmity could not possibly intrude. He admitted that it was hard going for a long, weary while, what with the drudging daily exercises and the slowness of improvement; but in time his mind took full command, and courage became a habit of life.

How well Franklin Roosevelt succeeded is now history. Stricken in the very prime of stalwart manhood, and seemingly through with public affairs except as an onlooker, he rose from his bed of suffering to become governor of New York and then President of the United States. Not merely for one term or two, but for a third and a fourth, overturning what had been regarded as an inviolable precedent since the time of George Washington. And it is to be remembered that not one of his administrations was without its incessant strain on mind, body, and soul. First a press of tremendous domestic problems, involving the country's social and economic reconstruction, and then the crushing burdens of leadership in a second World War.

What made the struggle more remarkable was the background of the man. Had he been a weakling, born puny and used to illness, patience and fortitude might have been expected. Instead of that, health was a birthright, and in his young manhood he could have posed for the sculptors of ancient Greece as they carved their heroes out of virgin marble. As a youngster he lived in the open, riding, climbing, running, sailing; and at Harvard he rowed on the crew and played football. Until his thirty-ninth year, in fact, he gloried in a strength and vigor that defied fatigue.

All of his earlier intimates stress his love of life and an incessant energy that took no account of body strain. His idea of a rest was a change of activity, a switch from one eager interest to another. No one, as near as I can discover, ever heard him admit weariness. Of many stories of his tirelessness, his love of movement, I like best Colonel Harry Roosevelt's melancholy tale of a visit that F. D. R. made to Haiti when he was Assistant Secretary of the Navy.

"I was in charge of a detachment of Marines at the time," Harry told me, "and when Frank arrived, everybody thought that it would be the usual tour of inspection, meaning dinners and receptions. And what happened? Racing through the official routine in jig-time, he dragged us off for a cross-country hike, on fire to see the life of the people and learn about the resources of the little republic. Our tramp from Port au Prince to Cap Haitien carried us over rugged mountain ranges, and daily marches were from dawn to dark.

"Reaching the north coast, all of us more dead than alive, we came to the old castle of Emperor Christophe, perched high on top of a four-thousand-foot peak. When the Secretary announced that he was going to climb the steep ascent, he did have the heart to call for volunteers, and two-thirds of the party had sense enough to refuse. I was one of the dumbbell

7

third, and while Frank came down as fresh as he started, the rest of us staggered to bed."

With such a past to look back on, Franklin Roosevelt might well have experienced revolt against his helplessness or felt a pang of bitter envy when he saw others engaging in sports that he had loved, and from which he was now forever barred. From the testimony of his family and my own observation, I can say truthfully that no one ever saw him indulge in so much as a moment of self-pity. Periods of depression, if any, were hidden and never at any time shadowed the smile with which he faced the future.

During his Navy years in Washington, he had turned to golf for exercise, and at Warm Springs I always had a bit of heartache when he followed our gang around the course in his car. It did not seem possible that he could watch unmoved, and yet as he jeered bad shots, and cheered good ones, it was as gaily as though he himself had a club in hand. In no sense was it a pose, but a mental attitude achieved by the force of his iron will.

Although he never recovered the full use of his legs, I think even that might have come about in large measure but for the war years, when the pressure forced him to neglect his daily regimen. In 1937 progress had been so continuous that he walked one hundred yards with only the arm of an attendant for support. As far as his upper body was concerned, however, he developed it to a degree that would have

8

shamed a heavyweight champion. In the White House pool he could outswim any of us, and when it came to fishing, he was easily the master.

Once off Cocos Island he hooked a 235-pound shark with medium tackle and landed it after a battle that lasted exactly one hour and a half. It was an exhibition of strength and endurance without parallel when it is considered that he had no legs with which to brace himself, and depended entirely on arms and shoulder muscles. And that was in 1940 after eight hard White House years.

During the third administration, however, improvement in his physical condition came to a full stop. He did not go back, but neither did he go forward. With American boys sailing to fight and die in far lands, the President lost all consideration of self. Nights as well as days were given over to conferences; and often, for weeks at a time, he skipped the daily routine so vital to his well-being. A bitter sacrifice, for he had looked forward with such eagerness to the day when he could throw away his braces, but made uncomplainingly.

It is entirely natural, of course, that present discussion should be principally concerned with Franklin Roosevelt's policies and the official acts of his four administrations. It is not only that many of them are still live issues and highly controversial, but in a democracy the political struggle is never adjourned. It is equally inevitable that historians will devote major attention to the history that he made, both in peace and war. Nevertheless, it would be nothing short of tragedy if Roosevelt the President pushed Roosevelt the *man* out of mind and memory. Maybe my own love and admiration incline me to exaggeration, but with all my heart I believe that no life—certainly none in our time—was more instinct with bravery of spirit, so rich in inspiration, or better fitted to serve as a pattern and an example for the handicapped of the world.

Now that there is a letdown from the intense emotionalism of war, when every citizen was keyed to service and sacrifice, there is a distinctly *whiny* note in the voice of America. With all of us picking up old threads and finding them sadly tangled, there is a very perceptible tendency to mean irritations and pettiness of soul. May it not be that a chronicle of courage and gallantry will have value in this dreary time?

My own experience as White House physician justifies the hope. Scarcely a day passed that men and women did not write to tell what the President's fight against infirmity had meant to them. These unsolicited testimonials still keep coming, and only recently I received a letter from Frederick L. Rath, Jr., a member of the National Park Service staff now administering the Hyde Park memorial. In it he gave this account of a talk with an employee who had known and watched Franklin Roosevelt in the summer after Campobello:

The man in question was employed in 1922 on the adjoining Morgan estate and he was telling me how F.D.R. would come over there on a three-wheel bicycle with no coaster brake. Mr. Roosevelt would allow himself to be pushed, thus exercising his legs. My informant also told me how F.D.R. tried horseback riding and how parallel bars were set up on the south porch of the home, high enough so that he could swing hand over hand with his toes just touching the porch floor, thus giving some motion to his legs and hips. We talked on for a while, but this old onlooker summed it up neatly and effectively when he said in admiration, "You know, if he had guts enough to fight like that, he was good enough for my money."

More important, what of the countless thousands maimed by war and compelled to start civilian careers under cruel handicaps? Young men who have lost their arms, their eyes, or their legs, and therefore are miles behind scratch in the race that faces them. Speaking as a physician, I insist that the story of Franklin Roosevelt's victorious struggle against infirmity holds the promise of benefits that rank with medicines and surgical care. This is not hopeful thinking but a factual statement based on personal observation.

On all of his trips the President never failed to visit the hospitals, no matter how crowded the day and regardless of his own fatigue. It was an unchanging ritual in the war zones as well as at home and not the dangers of Casablanca or Aleutian storms ever held him back. Nor were they casual, hurried tours done as a duty. He wheeled through every ward, stopping at bedsides for chats, maybe a pat on the back, his voice as warmly affectionate as though the broken soldiers and sailors were his own sons. Always there was a kindling of new light in dull, despairing eyes.

Two incidents that will ever stand out sharply in my memory took place in the summer of 1944 during his journey to the Pacific for conferences with General MacArthur and Admiral Nimitz. The stay in Hawaii was exhausting, for aside from the day and night discussions the President had inspected every war installation on the islands and had even gone deep into the jungle where men were training for Far Pacific fighting. It was at the end of a particularly full day that he climbed to the naval hospital in Aiea, high on the heights above Pearl Harbor, and filled at the time with some five thousand wounded veterans from Guam, Tinian, and Saipan.

Some 1,800 cases were being handled in the orthopedic wards, and these, very naturally, excited his deepest interest. A Marine lieutenant, smashed by mortar fire on Saipan, had actually helped to complete the amputation of his own leg while lying on the battlefield. The President was told of this, and on entering the room, held out his hand and beamed the broadest of his famous smiles. "Good morning, Doctor," he said. "I understand that you are quite a surgeon. Well, I happen to be a pretty good orthopedist myself, so what about a consultation?" It did not need a trained eye to see that boy's instant lift of spirit.

12

Soon afterward I happened to be walking ahead, and halted for a few words with a Marine who did not seem to have a whole bone left in his body. His face, ravaged by pain, was set in lines of utter dejection, but when he looked around and saw who was approaching, the youngster's mouth flew open in the widest and most delighted grin I have ever seen. "Gee!" he exclaimed. *"The President!"* So it was down the whole long line of beds in every ward. Not one of us but felt, actually *felt,* the wave of hope that swept the hospital as shattered men saw before them not merely the President of the United States but another human being, once struck down as they themselves were stricken, who had triumphed over physical disability by force of will and invincibility of spirit.

It is the memory of that day, and many other days when I saw the simple presence of Franklin Roosevelt work a similar miracle of encouragement, that has led me to set down this record of my more than twelve years of service as White House physician in daily attendance on a great and gallant soul.

CHAPTER II

HOW WELL WAS THE PRESIDENT?

DURING THE 1932 CAMPAIGN A WHISPER WENT THE rounds that poliomyelitis had left Franklin Roosevelt in such physical condition that, if elected, he could not possibly stand the strain of the presidential office. This vicious whisper had a long life and only died a lingering death when conclusive proofs of his perfect health and well-nigh incredible vitality made the charge increasingly absurd.

In the 1944 campaign, when lost weight, thinning hair, and heavily furrowed face all too plainly showed the toll taken by crowded years, rumors as to his condition revived and had the sweep of a prairie fire. It became "common knowledge," according to wagging tongues, that the President had suffered a paralytic stroke, that he was being treated for cancer of the prostate, that he was the victim of a mental breakdown, and, favorite whisper of all, that his heart had played out. Time and again it was specifically asserted that he was in a hospital for some major operation, although

14

there was never any agreement on the city. One whisper said Miami, and another Chicago.

In not one of these rumors was there a grain of truth. The President never had a stroke, never had any serious heart condition, and never underwent other operations than the removal of a wen and the extraction of an infected tooth. As an illustration of the utter baselessness of these whispering campaigns, and also the manner in which they start and spread, I cite the confession of one gossiper that we were able to run down. The information that led to his detection came in a letter to the President from an anxious woman living in a western state. A certain doctor, she wrote, was busily circulating the report that the President suffered from a malignant malady for which there was no cure. Although he said that he knew it to be so from his own personal observation, she had her doubts and wanted to know the truth.

The letter was given to an investigatory agency of government, and the garrulous doctor was asked for an explanation. He broke down under questioning and admitted that he had merely repeated hearsay, embroidering it with colorful touches of his own. There was no malice in it, as far as could be determined, but only a cheap vanity that made him try to appear as "high up and inside." It also happened to be the case that the doctor had friends who were close to the White House, and they begged the President to let the matter drop, assuring him that the doctor had learned his lesson. This was done in spite of strong protests from close friends, for there was a general feeling that public prosecution would have had a good effect on loose, irresponsible mouths.

Today, however, as a result of the President's sudden death, there is a growing conviction that these rumors had a base in solid fact. In writing of Teheran and Yalta, it has become the fixed habit of many editors and columnists to state without qualification that Franklin Roosevelt was a sick man, even a dying man, in the last year of his life. On the strength of this assumption, I am adjudged as having deliberately deceived the people of the United States by the issuance of statements that the President was sound organically and in fairly good health.

Through all of the years of his White House occupancy the President was given an annual examination similar to those demanded by the Navy of its officer personnel. Before a journey of any duration we went over him from head to foot, and again on his return. Particularly was this the case with respect to the Casablanca, Teheran, and Yalta conferences, all putting a heavy strain on his reserves. In 1943, 1944, and the months in 1945 just prior to his passing, checkups were frequent and exhaustive. It was on the strength of those repeated examinations, made under my direction by competent specialists, and on the basis of reports rendered by distinguished consultants, that I

16

issued my statements to the press in the spring and fall of 1944.

I did not volunteer these statements but gave them when personally and pointedly queried by the Washington correspondents. They were not "glowing" in the sense that they painted the President as a perfect physical specimen, but a cautious judgment that he was in "excellent condition for a man of his age." *I stand by that judgment today without amendment or apology.* Although he was tired and worn, since he could not be induced to spare himself, every check justified the expectation that he could and would continue to carry the load, barring the unforeseen.

All of these examinations are of record, but they would fill many large volumes, besides being repetitive and phrased in medical terminology. In later chapters I will deal with them in considerable detail; but here at the outset let me skim over my twelve years as White House physician, summarizing the President's physical condition in language that the layman can understand.

Franklin Roosevelt's first complete going-over, after my appointment, took place in November 1933. As I was an eye, ear, nose, and throat man, other specialists were called in. Apart from his legs, the examination showed him to be in exceptionally good shape for one entering his fifties. Weight 190, chest development far above average, blood pressure normal, no anemia, and not a sign of any organic defect. All in

17

all, a patient that would not cause any great amount of worry.

From the day that he was stricken in 1921, Mr. Roosevelt had made a profound study of his case, and the system of exercises worked out by himself had resulted in marked improvement. Consultants saw no reason to suggest changes, and my agreement with him on a set of rules for daily living involved no radical departures. My one insistence, in view of the burdens of the presidency, was that he should get away from the White House every three or four months. I would have given this advice had he been whole in every respect.

Going over the reports for 1934 and 1935, I find few variations, and the campaign of 1936, while entailing added strain, left no evidence of lessened vitality. In the spring of 1937 the President experienced an attack of influenza that kept him away from his desk for a week or so, but he soon regained complete fitness, and checks on the heart, chest, and other vital functioning organs were satisfactory.

The examinations throughout 1938 and 1939 were routine, likewise those made in 1940. The strenuous campaign, plus the anxieties stirred by the international situation, produced no perceptible impairment. In 1941, however, the President suffered another attack of intestinal influenza, as well as a complicating factor of internal hemorrhoids. This gave us some

18

concern, but by June he presented a perfectly normal picture.

Our entrance into the war brought a crushing increase in work and strain, and the presence of German submarines in the Atlantic also precluded the fishing trips that had done so much to keep the President in trim. As a result, there came a definite halt in the steady gains that had been made in building up his muscular structure. Not deterioration but a standstill in improvement. From that time on my problem, quite frankly, was to protect his reserves. The one change in the daily schedule, however, was a slowing-down in all forms of exercise, although the President himself protested, seeing no reason for it.

Despite the additional output of energy in 1941 and 1942, I had small cause for complaint. Any indisposition soon disappeared, for he still possessed the necessary stamina to come back quickly from an attack of the grippe, a sinus flare-up, or the absorption of infection from a tooth. His blood pressure remained on an excellent level; his kidney and liver functions were normal, and his cardiovascular measurements were within normal standards for a man of his age. His weight continued to vary between 185 and 192 pounds.

In January 1943, prior to the Casablanca conference, a particularly thorough examination was made, not only because of the expected strain but by reason of the fact that he had determined to fly across the

Atlantic. The tests won our consent to the trip by air, as they demonstrated that the President had an excellent ceiling. The blood-pressure readings were well within a most satisfying range; and his response to exercise, from the standpoint of the heart, was all that could be wished. A complete checkup in November 1943, prior to the Teheran trip, showed virtually no change from the findings in January.

I think, therefore, we can assume general agreement that the President's physical condition held no cause for alarm up to Teheran. After ten years in office, all packed to the brim with tasks that imposed incessant strain, he showed no other ill effects than a small loss of weight and a few more care lines.

Teheran, according to our check, marked the resumption of operations by the rumor factories. From that time until the day of his death, malignant whisperings swept through the land from coast to coast. Our records prove that they had no solid ground. The President's journeying covered 17,742 sea, land, and air miles, with stops in Cairo, Malta, and Sicily as well as Teheran, but when he landed back in Washington on December 17, every test proved him to be in good physical condition. He was tired, to be sure, for 1943 was an exhausting year, but still possessed his remarkable ability to pick up when given a short break between activities.

It was not Teheran, but the post-Teheran period, that worked the change that gave cause for anxiety.

Going to Hyde Park for Christmas, he contracted influenza and experienced several attacks of acute respiratory infection in the weeks that followed. Along with these he suffered short spells of abdominal distress and distension, accompanied by profuse perspiration. Constant coughing robbed him of restful sleep; and one day found him up, and the next day down.

To lessen the heart load as much as possible, it was decided to bring about a gradual reduction in weight, taking off ten pounds by a decrease in diet. Although necessary and helpful, the measure had hurtful consequences eventually, for the President took such pride in his flat stomach that he began to cut down on his food, going beyond the dietary requirements prescribed. All through March I made every effort to get him to quit the grind for a while, but it was not until April 8 that he consented to go to South Carolina for a complete rest.

In a later chapter I am including a complete report on the stay at Bernie Baruch's plantation, for it was during this period that the most alarming reports as to the President's physical condition were given circulation. I felt then, however, and still feel, that doubts as to his recovery should have been dissipated by his intense and unceasing activity throughout the rest of the year. In midsummer there was the journey to Hawaii for the important conferences with General MacArthur and Admiral Nimitz, after which he went to the stormy, fog-bound Aleutians. In September came the Quebec meeting with Prime Minister Churchill, and then, with scarce a pause for breath, the President plunged into his campaign for re-election.

I submit that a sick and failing man could not have stood these arduous journeys, calling for mental as well as physical effort, as well as the expenditure of energy required by many back-platform speeches and major addresses in New York, Boston, and Chicago. I said then, and I say now, that the President came through the campaign in a manner that justified my earlier predictions. For those who doubt, I have been at pains to set down the checkups made throughout this period and attested by reputable physicians. (See Chapter XV.)

The gossipers, in fact, were never further from the truth than when they declared that the President's "collapse" was plainly apparent both before and during the campaign. It was the period between election day and the inauguration that justified concern. There was a press of domestic problems that called for quick solution, and also the leaden weight of an involved international situation. Aside from Russia's "go it alone" and "none of your business" attitude with respect to Poland and other conquered countries, Marshal Stalin showed small inclination to join in the war against Japan. Worse still, he refused to commit himself as to the United Nations, F. D. R.'s creation and the thing closest to his heart.

Driving himself as never before, the President ate luncheons at his desk, surrounded by conferees; failed to take his afternoon rest and worked far into each night. January 20 found him tired to an extent that displeased us all, but with his usual show of will he delivered his inaugural address in an acceptable manner. The Yalta trip, like many others that preceded it, was a "must"; and it was one that we did not look forward to with any great pleasure as the President was tired. The prospect, however, of a trip at sea made me feel that he would again rebound from the fatigued condition in which he found himself. As I have said many times before, my best measure of the President's condition was his ability to come back quickly when he was tired. The voyage from Norfolk to Malta gave me an opportunity to see whether this would be the case; and the ten days needed to make the Atlantic crossing, and the run up the Mediterranean to Malta, did just that.

Aside from the highly controversial nature of the Yalta conference, due to profound differences of opinion among the Big Three, there were the interminable dinners with their endless Russian menus, that necessitated late hours. Each evening found the President very tired, but after a light massage he slept well, and the mornings found him refreshed and ready for the day's routine. From first to last he ate with good appetite, relishing the simpler dishes, and actually put on weight.

23

Had he been "dying on his feet" at Yalta, I, as one bound by his professional oath, could not and would not have permitted the President to have poured out his energy in day and night sessions. Nor would I have given my consent to the long and fatiguing post-Yalta itinerary. (See Chapter XVII.) The six-hour flight to Egypt was over mountain ranges from eight to eleven thousand feet in height, and the conferences at Great Bitter Lake were continuous and exhausting. Nevertheless, the correspondents on board all bore testimony to the President's fitness.

I had hoped for rest and complete relaxation on the homeward voyage, but it did not turn out that way. Instead of sleeping late and lounging in the sun, the President began work at once on his Yalta report. And then, with tragic suddenness, came the death of General Watson, his military aide and cherished friend. It was a blow that shook him, for Pa had been as dear to him as his own flesh and blood.

For all his air of encompassing friendliness, the President was slow to give affection; and those that he took to his heart of hearts were held with hooks of steel. One by one he had lost those who were closest to him and on whom he most depended. Louis Howe, Marvin McIntyre, "Missy" Le Hand, Dan Callaghan, Frank Knox, his Secretary of the Navy, Rudolph Forster, stout Gus Gennerich, on whose arm he had leaned for so long a time, and gay, loyal Pa.

Now began the most trying period of all my years in

the White House. With the first meeting of the United Nations set for April in San Francisco, the President bent every energy to perfecting plans for its success. With Hitler at bay and MacArthur and Nimitz preparing for final blows in the Pacific, there were continuous conferences with his military advisers. When I protested against the manner in which he was driving himself, he simply answered that there was "just so much to be done, and just so much time in which to do it. We must bring this war to an end."

The results of overwork and nervous strain were soon apparent. Again there was the complaint that nothing "tasted right," and loss of appetite cost him more precious pounds. Examinations in March (see Chapter XVIII) proved heart and lungs to be in good condition, and blood-pressure values were considerably lower. In conversation with him I made no effort to conceal my concern, and told him flatly that only a complete rest could prevent collapse. He came back, as usual, with the answer that every checkup showed him to be organically sound, but I knocked over this argument by stressing the toxic effects of fatigue.

It was not only the San Francisco conference that he planned to attend; arrangements were already in the making for a flight to London, and after that a visit to the Far Pacific to see the finish of the war with Japan. When I told him that not even the San Francisco trip would be possible unless he put on ten pounds at the very least, he grudgingly consented to go to Warm Springs.

As will be seen by my detailed account of the President's last days, reports were encouraging up to the very moment of his passing. Keeping to the promise he had given me, he saw few visitors and rested well. His appetite improved to a point where he was taking double helpings, adding eight pounds to his weight. By April 6 he was going out in his car for long afternoon drives; and he began to take up his paper work, or his "wash," as he called the routine drudgery of reading and signing endless documents.

The President's heart reserve was what we were guarding, and on the morning of April 18, Dr. Bruenn gave me a most satisfactory report. The diastolic pressure was at 88, the level held through the years, and after a hearty breakfast that he enjoyed, the patient seemed in high spirits. The end, therefore, came with shocking suddenness. One moment talking and laughing with members of his staff, and the next slumped in his chair, pale, cold, and unconscious.

Dr. Paullin, racing from Atlanta, went into immediate consultation with Dr. Bruenn, and there was a brief while when it seemed that the President's recuperative powers might prevail. Both physicians were in complete agreement that the cause of death was a "massive cerebral hemorrhage," as all of the signs and symptoms from the beginning of unconsciousness to the end presented a textbook picture for this condition.

So the efforts to work out methods that would protect the President until the completion of his task had failed. The heart that we feared for carried its load to the very last. Once again we were brought to the realization that there are many conditions that medical science does not disclose. One of our leading pathologists has analyzed more than three hundred cases of cerebral hemorrhage in the hope of finding definite signs that would enable the doctor to discern the danger to his patient in advance, but up to now only theory is available.

Dr. Bruenn has recorded his observations on the President's physical condition during the latter part of his life and has kindly allowed me to quote these impressions of a skilled and keen observer:

It was my good fortune to be with the President for almost two years before he died. Because of this, a valid basis of comparison exists for me. There is no question but that the President was physically tired. The crushing burdens of the war and the domestic front, together with an election campaign in the preceding months had sapped his strength. Yet he made the journey to Yalta in February 1945 in extraordinarily good fashion. This trip, you will recall, employed practically all forms of transportation known to man, except possibly oxcarts. And at Yalta he gave freely of his time not only to the main conferences, but also devoted himself to the encouragement and advice

27

of the several members of the party in their individual responsibilities.

Despite the demands made upon him, his mental clarity was truly remarkable. His memory for past and recent events was unimpaired and his recollection of detail was such as to continually impress me when compared with some of his associates ten and twenty years younger than himself. His vitality and sense of humor remained excellent and only on one occasion, if you remember, did I see him depressed, i.e., when the Russians were proving to be more difficult than usual. The morning afterwards, however, he was his usual buoyant self.

The return trip proved to be most enjoyable, and he seemed to relax and rest so that I felt much relieved about him. He was greatly saddened, as were we all, by the death of "Pa" Watson, but his tremendous character enabled him to take this shock without faltering.

It was not infrequently his custom, when he retired at night, to relax and speak in very general terms of events and people. During the last six weeks of his life, his trend of thought, his appraisal of situations and his evaluation of circumstances were just as clear and keen as they ever had been. He was always several steps ahead of his contemporaries and he maintained this superiority to the end. I can recall one incident which might illustrate this. The overwhelming wish of the President at this time was for an enduring peace and a workable United Nations. He was insistent upon going to the West Coast on April 25, 1945, for the first meeting of the United Nations. All of us pleaded with him not to make the trip because of the stress of a trans-continental journey for the purpose of making a fifteen minute speech. It was suggested that if his presence were needed later, he might then go. He

finally explained why he felt that the trip must be made
as he had planned. He hoped, he said, that by starting
the Conference off on the right note, it might accomplish
its purposes more readily. Whereas if he were to appear
later in case difficulties should arise at the meeting, it
would appear to be unilateral action on his part.

The speech which he had prepared by his own hand
for presentation at the Conference in San Francisco was
written just a few days before he died. All doubt as to
the man's mental powers can be answered in its expression
of purpose, conciseness of phraseology and stirring appeal.
I truly believe that had he been spared, this nation and
the world would now be immeasurably further along the
road to a lasting peace and a mutual respect and understanding.

CHAPTER III

UP FROM INVALIDISM

COMING ON THE SCENE SOME TEN YEARS AFTER MR. Roosevelt's affliction, I had no firsthand knowledge of the struggle throughout that trying period. From Mrs. Roosevelt, Louie Howe, Missy Le Hand, and others of the family circle, however, I gained a clear picture of what he, and they themselves, had been called on to endure. The President, in the course of our consultations as to his care and treatment, also made contributions now and then, although he had small liking for remembrance.

For example, he never once mentioned a remarkable letter that he wrote from Warm Springs, under date of October 11, 1924, to Dr. William Eggleston of Hartsville, South Carolina. Had Mrs. Eggleston not given it to the *Journal of the South Carolina Medical Association* for publication in the spring of 1946, I would have known nothing of it. I am reprinting it in full, not only as a case report but because of its warm, human value:

Please excuse my delay in replying to your letter which has been forwarded to me down here in your neighboring state where I am spending a few weeks swimming and getting sunlight for my legs. I am very glad to tell you what I can in regard to my case and as I have talked it over with a great many doctors can, I think, give you a history of the case which would be equal to theirs.

First symptoms of the illness appeared in August, 1921, when I was thoroughly tired from overwork. I first had a chill in the evening which lasted practically all night. The following morning the muscles of the right knee appeared weak and by afternoon I was unable to support my weight on my right leg. That evening the left knee began to weaken also and by the following morning I was unable to stand up. This was accompanied by a continuing temperature of about 102 and I felt thoroughly achy all over. By the end of the third day practically all muscles from the chest down were involved. Above the chest the only symptom was a weakening of the two large thumb muscles making it impossible to write. There was no special pain along the spine and no rigidity of the neck.

For the following two weeks I had to be catheterized and there was slight, though not severe, difficulty in controlling the bowels. The fever lasted for only 6 or 7 days, but all the muscles from the hips down were extremely sensitive to the touch and I had to have the knees supported by pillows. This condition of extreme discomfort lasted about 3 weeks. I was then moved to a New York hospital and finally moved home in November, being able by that time to sit up in a wheel chair, but the leg muscles remained extremely sensitive and this sensitive-

31

ness disappeared gradually over a period of six months, the last remaining point being the calf muscles.

As to treatment—the mistake was made for the first 10 days of giving my feet and lower legs rather heavy massage. This was stopped by Dr. Lovett, of Boston, who was, without doubt, the greatest specialist on infantile paralysis. In January, 1922, 5 months after the attack, he found that the muscles behind the knees had contracted and that there was a tendency to foot-drop in the right foot. These were corrected by the use of plaster casts during two weeks. In February, 1922, braces were fitted on each leg from the hips to the shoes, and I was able to stand up and learned gradually to walk with crutches. At the same time gentle exercises were begun, first every other day, then daily, exercising each muscle 10 times and seeking to avoid any undue strain by giving each muscle the correct movement with gravity. These exercises I did on a board placed on the bed.

The recovery of muscle paralysis began at this time, though for many months it seemed to make little progress. In the summer of 1922 I began swimming and found that this exercise seemed better adapted than any other because all weight was removed from the legs and I was able to move the legs in the water far better than I had expected. Since that time, i.e., for the last two years, I have as far as possible, in connection with my work and other duties, carried out practically the same treatment with the result that the muscles have increased in power to a remarkable extent and the improvement in the past 6 months has been even more rapid than at any previous time.

32

I still wear braces, of course, because the quadriceps are not yet strong enough to bear my weight. One year ago I was able to stand in fresh water without braces when the water was up to my chin. Six months ago I could stand in water up to the top of my shoulders and today can stand in water just level with my arm pits. This is a very simple method for me of determining how fast the quadriceps are coming back. Aside from these muscles the waist muscles on the right side are still weak and the outside muscles on the right leg have strengthened so much more than the inside muscles that they pull my right foot forward. I continue corrective exercises for all the muscles.

To sum up I would give you the following "Don'ts":

Don't use heavy massage but use light massage rubbing always towards the heart.

Don't let the patient over-exercise any muscle or get tired.

Don't let the patient feel cold, especially the legs, feet or any other part affected. Progress stops entirely when the legs or feet are cold.

Don't let the patient get too fat.

The following treatment is so far the best, judging from my own experience and that of hundreds of other cases which I have studied:

1. Gentle exercise especially for the muscles which seem to be worst affected.

2. Gentle skin rubbing—not muscle kneading—bearing in mind that good circulation is a prime requisite.

33

3. Swimming in warm water—lots of it.

4. Sunlight—all the patient can get, especially direct sunlight on the affected parts. It would be ideal to lie in the sun all day with nothing on. This is difficult to accomplish but the nearest approach to it is a bathing suit.

5. Belief on the patient's part that the muscles are coming back and will eventually regain recovery of the affected parts. There are cases known in Norway where adults have taken the disease and not been able to walk until after a lapse of 10 or even 12 years.

I hope that your patient has not got a very severe case. They all differ, of course, in the degree in which the parts are affected. If braces are necessary there is a man in New York, whose name I will send you, if you wish, when I get back to New York, who makes remarkable light braces of duraluminum. My first braces of steel weighed 7 lbs. apiece—my new ones weigh only 4 lbs. apiece. Remember that braces are only for the convenience of the patient in getting around—a leg in a brace does not have a chance for muscle development. This muscle development must come through exercise when the brace is not on—such as swimming, etc.

Very truly yours,
Franklin D. Roosevelt

I agree with the editor of the *Journal* that the letter will become "one of the famous case reports of medical history." At the time of writing, the treatment of polio was largely a matter of trial and error. There was no appreciation of the value of heat, and few doctors realized the necessity of protecting damaged muscles and guarding against undue exercise. Franklin Roosevelt, intelligent and tireless, blazed new trails.

From such letters and through questioning, I came to the conviction that his superabundant energy, a belief in his own invulnerability, opened the door to infantile paralysis. The record, in my opinion, proves it. After eight crowded years as Assistant Secretary of the Navy, a rest was plainly indicated, but before Mr. Roosevelt could resign, the Democrats gave him the vice-presidential nomination in 1920 as James M. Cox's running mate.

Too much of a realist to fool himself, he knew from the start that the ticket was doomed to defeat, but he leaped at the chance to declare his faith in the League of Nations, and campaigned from coast to coast as enthusiastically as though victory were assured. After the election he turned to his personal affairs, so long neglected, and formed a law firm that occupied him unceasingly throughout the winter, spring, and early summer. It was not until August that he joined the family in Campobello, his summer home in Canada, and although confessing that he felt a "little tired," followed his usual practice of making no concession to fatigue.

On the day that he was stricken, for example, he and the children had spent the forenoon sailing. On the way back all stopped to help beat out a forest fire,

35

and it was four o'clock before they reached home. Deciding that a dip would buck him up, Mr. Roosevelt first swam around in a little landlocked lake and then took a plunge in the icy waters of the Bay of Fundy. Dogtrotting the two miles to the house, he then sat down in his wet clothes to go over the mail.

The days that followed were ones that all of the Roosevelts tried to forget. There were weary weeks in the hospital and then weeks at home when he lay in heavy casts that stretched the muscles. Each day a little of the plaster was chipped out at the back, adding to the pull; but, while those who loved him were often in tears, he bore the torture uncomplainingly and with never a break in his cheerful fortitude. By summer he had progressed sufficiently to insist on crutches, and in the quiet of Hyde Park he spent many pain-filled hours patiently performing exercises designed to strengthen his legs. There for the first time, in a small outdoor pool, he tried swimming, later on to prove such an important factor in his recovery.

Even before the end of his convalescent period Mr. Roosevelt set about the fulfillment of his pledge never to accept invalidism. Resuming his duties as vice-president of the Fidelity and Deposit Company, he also took the presidency of the American Reconstruction Council, a clearinghouse for the building industry. Going further, he interested himself in the Boy Scouts and headed the movement for the purchase of an eleven-thousand-acre scout center in Sullivan County.

Moreover, under the steady urging of Louis McHenry Howe, he began to manifest a concern in national affairs.

I do not believe there was ever a more devoted friendship than that which began in 1910 when the gnarled, cynical little Albany correspondent for a New York newspaper dedicated his life to the tall, handsome, athletic young state senator. No two men were ever more dissimilar, both as to background and personality, and yet they sustained a Damon and Pythias relationship to the last, with Louie the only one of the inner circle privileged to call the President by his first name.

When Mr. Roosevelt went to Washington in 1913 as Assistant Secretary of the Navy, Howe accompanied him and sat at his right hand. After the unsuccessful campaign of 1920 Louie planned to go back to his profession; but, when news came of the Campobello tragedy, he dropped everything and became a member of the Roosevelt household. As much as Mrs. Roosevelt herself, he aided the fight for recovery, holding fast to a passionate conviction that his idol was destined for greatness.

The presidential candidacy of Alfred Smith in 1924 enlisted Franklin Roosevelt's enthusiastic support, and the Democratic National Convention offered dramatic opportunity for his first public appearance. As he hobbled on crutches to the platform in Madison Square Garden, and made the stirring "Happy Warrior" speech that placed the Governor in nomination, even opposed delegations cheered him for his courage.

During the summer, as F. D. R. plugged away at his exercises in Hyde Park, George Foster Peabody, the banker and philanthropist, wrote him about an old health resort he had just bought in western Georgia. The pool, its chief feature, had a temperature of 89°, and a very high specific gravity due to double molecules of magnesium and calcium. Mr. Peabody reported that victims of infantile paralysis had received marked benefits from bathing in the waters. I myself can bear similar testimony, for I have seen a helpless child, unable to move an arm, get real motion when placed in the pool. Aside from the regeneration of the injured muscle groups, there was the tremendous rise in the youngster's morale.

Considerably impressed, the Roosevelts went to Warm Springs that fall, renting one of the dilapidated cottages that surrounded the ancient frame hotel. A more forlorn place could not have been imagined, but the pool justified everything that Mr. Peabody had said about it. Little was known about the cause and cure of polio at the time, and there was not even a doctor at hand, but with his usual determination Mr. Roosevelt set about evolving his own method of treatment.

Day after day, hour after hour, he experimented, teaching himself to use his legs in the water and struggling to get his feet down and walk on the bottom.

Along with swimming, he clung to the sides of the pool and went through exercises that stretched the damaged muscles. Parts of a letter that he wrote to Mr. Peabody at the time are well worth quoting, for not only do they show the dawn of his own hope but the beginning of an interest in others suffering from the same affliction:

Every morning I spend two hours in the most wonderful pool in the world, and it is no exaggeration to say that the muscles in my legs have improved to an extent noticeable in every way.... Swimming and sunlight combined constitute the best remedy for the restoration of the muscles.... Infantile paralysis is, unfortunately, now one of the great epidemic diseases of the U. S. Dr. Lovett, who was the greatest specialist in this, told me that he expected from now on there would be sporadic epidemics every year, and a major epidemic every six or seven years. As no preventive or serum has been discovered, this means that there will be thousands of cripples, not only among children, but also among adults. Nothing finer or more useful to humanity could be done than to establish a "cure" where the best of treatment along the lines of the accepted treatment could be given.

The test of the sincerity of this interest in fellow sufferers was not long in coming. The reporter for an Atlanta paper, hearing about Franklin Roosevelt's enthusiasm, visited Warm Springs in search of a feature, and his article, "Swimming Back to Health," went all over the country. As a result, victims of infantile paralysis began heading for Georgia from every section,

39

crowding the ancient resort far beyond its capacity. Many were without funds, and all pathetic in their hope of a miracle that would make them whole and strong.

As F. D. R. himself admitted to me, the invasion marked a turning point in his life. The old hotel was totally inadequate, and there was no medical attendance or nurses. Moreover, the influx constituted a very definite interference with his own comfort and progress. Since he was under no obligation to any of the newcomers, he could have let them mill around unhappily for a while and then go away.

Such a course might possibly have been followed by the gay, unthinking Harvard student or the handsome, popular Assistant Secretary of the Navy with the world his oyster; but it did not enter the thought of the Franklin Roosevelt who had known suffering and agony of spirit. Cheerfully, compassionately, he helped to house and feed the newcomers. Every day he explained the stretching treatment that he had devised for himself, and even personally directed the water exercises that had worked such marked improvement in his own case.

In 1934, at a Thanksgiving Day party given for his fellow patients, the President touched intimately on some of those early experiences. "During that first year," he reminisced, "I was doctor and physiotherapist rolled into one. On returning in 1926, and finding that more sufferers had arrived, we managed to arrange for adequate medical supervision. Housing, however, remained a problem, and along with the care of patients, we toiled at running a hotel. A five-piece band also represented a gamble of magnitude, for our financial resources only justified three pieces."

Increasingly convinced of the curative value of the waters and eager to have the largest possible numbers receive its benefits, Mr. Roosevelt began to dream of enlargement and improvement on a grand scale. In 1926 the Orthopedic Association happened to be holding its annual convention in Atlanta, and he drove over to ask these specialists for a consideration of Warm Springs and its possibilities. After some hemming and hawing a committee was appointed, and in due time it reported favorably.

That was all the enthusiast needed, and without more ado he bought the property from Mr. Peabody and incorporated the Georgia Warm Springs Foundation as a non-profit-making institution. About twelve hundred acres were taken over, together with the buildings. Fully two-thirds of his personal fortune went into the venture, and later demands required additional funds as he renovated, built, and equipped.

In my opinion nothing shows more clearly the deep humanity of the man than the Foundation's development. And, I might add, his very real administrative ability. For the first seven years it was a purely personal undertaking, for while friends and charitable organizations made contributions and put up memorial buildings, Franklin Roosevelt stood back of it all as guarantor. Not until 1934, when the first of the President's Birthday Balls netted $1,016,433, was the project put on a firm financial footing, ceasing to be his personal obligation. As a result, he ruled that only 30 per cent of the proceeds from the balls should be allotted to the Foundation in 1935, 1936, and 1937, letting 70 per cent remain in the communities where raised, for the aid of local sufferers from polio.

Even the burdens of the presidency brought no lessening of interest, and there were many occasions on which he made the future of the Foundation a subject of discussion. More and more, as the years went on, the conviction grew that treating the aftereffects of polio was not enough. The thing to do, he maintained, was to attack the whole problem through every kind of research, and that meant supplementing Warm Springs by the creation of a purely scientific body.

By 1938 the President's thought had taken shape, and he announced the incorporation of the National Foundation for Infantile Paralysis in this statement of purpose: "To lead, direct and unify the fight on every phase of this sickness. It will make every effort to ensure that every responsible research agency in this country is adequately financed to carry on investigations into the cause of infantile paralysis and the methods by which it may be prevented." Since 1938, therefore, Warm Springs has not shared in the money from the Birthday Balls, the net proceeds being

42

divided between the National Foundation and the communities.

Little Warm Springs, however, continued to be closest to the President's heart. The work of the National Foundation was fine and necessary, but it did not afford the human contacts that he loved. Down in Georgia, riding around the grounds and swimming in the pool with scores of others, he could see with his own eyes restorative processes at work. It delighted him to be stopped and asked for advice, and he loved the evenings when he talked of his experiences and poured out the wine of his courage. In the beginning I had a doubt as to whether it was good for him to be around sick people, but dismissed it when I saw the pleasure it gave him to be of service.

Shortly after America's entry into the war, and when he was driven to the limit of his reserves, the President sent for me and asked what plans had been made for taking care of such Navy personnel as might contract polio. When I told him that it was going to be difficult for our crowded hospitals to give the necessary treatment, he offered me an allotment of space in Warm Springs. Starting with ten beds, the number of patients increased until I was forced to beg room for the establishment of a Navy unit. As a result of the care afforded at Warm Springs, scores of young men and women in the Navy and Marine Corps are today enjoying normal, useful lives.

Warm Springs, to my mind, is the *real* monument to

Franklin Roosevelt. Others also contributed money and effort; but it was his guiding hand and compassionate heart that built up a run-down health resort into a great national institution, offering treatment to five and six hundred patients a year, regardless of race, creed, or ability to pay.

CHAPTER IV

RETURN TO PUBLIC LIFE

E VERYTHING ABOUT THE PRESIDENT WAS OF INTEREST to me and led to a good deal of questioning. Some of it, of course, came from a natural desire to learn the full story of an exciting life, but there was also the fact that a physician must know the mind of his patient as well as the body. Why had he done this and why had he done that? Fishing trips and plane and train rides afforded opportunities for long talks, and when in the mood, he liked nothing better than to reminisce. His return to public life, and that at a time when he looked to have a chance for fairly complete recovery, was one of the things that most interested me. Not all at once but in the course of many conversations, I gained the reasons both for his gubernatorial and presidential candidacies.

The start of it all was the "Happy Warrior" speech in 1924, for it gave notice that Franklin Roosevelt had no intention of watching public affairs from the side lines. Where the ball of his destiny really began to roll, however, was when he went to Houston in 1928 to place Governor Smith in nomination a second time. Again enthusiastic cheering paid a tribute to his indomitable spirit, and Democratic leaders sounded him out on his political plans. He told them frankly that he had none. Having discharged every obligation of loyalty both to his friend and his party, he went back to Warm Springs, resolved to devote himself to his recovery.

Not only did the movement to draft him for the New York gubernatorial race start without his knowledge, but it met with his instant and vigorous protest. At the time he was beginning to walk with only the aid of a cane, and his physicians assured him that if he kept up his swimming and exercises and avoided the cold northern winters, he might expect increasing improvement. To quit Warm Springs for the strain of a campaign might well mean the loss of all he had gained. His position was set forth clearly in the following telegram to Governor Smith:

Confirming my telephone message, I wish much that I might even consider the possibility of running for Governor this year, especially if by so doing I could further help you, but there are two considerations which are compelling.

First, your own record in New York State is so clear to the voters that you will carry the State regardless of who is nominated for Governor and my nomination would make no difference to your success on the New York ticket.

Secondly, my doctors are very definite in stating that the continued improvement in my condition is dependent on my avoidance of cold climate, and on taking exercises here at Warm Springs during the cold winter months. It probably means getting rid of leg braces during next two winters and that would be impossible if I had to remain in Albany. As I am only 46 years of age, I feel that I owe it to my family and myself to give the present constant improvement a chance to continue. I must therefore with great regret confirm my decision not to accept the nomination and I know you will understand.

Party leaders, however, redoubled their pressure, convinced that the Roosevelt candidacy would add strength to the national ticket, but it was Al Smith's personal plea that finally won his consent. Apart from a personal affection for the Governor, there was his admiration for one who had started from humble beginnings and worked his way up to the topmost rung of the American ladder. It was a feeling that did not change even when Governor Smith joined the ranks of the Liberty Leaguers and gave F.D.R. some pretty bitter tongue-lashings.

The consent was held back, however, until he had received assurance that the Warm Springs Foundation would suffer no hurt from what he regarded as his desertion. As I understood it, John J. Raskob and others guaranteed to keep the newly launched enterprise afloat. Only when he had been given this promise did Franklin Roosevelt let his name be put in nomination.

47

Once committed, he campaigned with a vigor that amazed his friends and astounded the opposition, for the supposed "cripple" made as many as fifteen speeches a day. And not the usual hack stuff, cautious in its generalities, but specific pledges as to what reforms he would institute and what evils he would correct. When the votes were counted, the returns showed him a winner, while Governor Smith was buried under the Hoover landslide, failing even to carry New York.

Election brought about the physical results that Franklin Roosevelt had feared, for the duties of office prevented further progress in recovery. Braces continued to be a necessity, and their weight distorted his muscles and put an increasing strain on his back. The Albany pool was a poor substitute for Warm Springs, and unable to find time for systematic exercises, he was forced to place increasing dependence on crutches.

What he had counted on was retirement after one term. Not only was the presidency *not* in his mind, but the political outlook convinced him that he would be defeated for re-election to the governorship. The sweep of the victory in 1928 had lifted the Republicans to a new high, and Democratic prospects seemed so hopeless that many prophesied the party's dissolution. President Hoover himself was sufficiently elated to prophesy a chicken in every pot and a car in every garage.

It was the crash of 1929 that changed the whole picture with startling suddenness. Renominated in 1930 by acclamation, Franklin Roosevelt went on to win by the unprecedented majority of 725,000. This was Louie Howe's great opportunity. From the day that he had hitched his wagon to the Roosevelt star, the idolatrous little man had dreamed of the time when his beloved Franklin would be President of the United States, and the overwhelming triumph was seen by him as a long step to the White House. Jim Farley was no less an enthusiast, and the two combined on the issuance of a postelection statement that made bold mention of Governor Roosevelt as the strongest possible Democratic candidate in 1932.

The suggestion met with a favorable reception throughout the country, and again, as in 1928, Mr. Roosevelt was faced with a momentous decision. First, there was the strain of a nation-wide campaign and, in event of victory, the burdens of a man-killing office. Clearly, inescapably, he saw that a declaration of candidacy meant the surrender of his hope for complete recovery, and pain-filled years of dependence on the braces that he hated.

As we sat together one evening in the White House years later, he told me of the considerations that had led him to yield to the insistence of Farley and Howe. The country lay prostrate under a weight of misery and fear, with courage and initiative no more than memories. The cause, in his opinion, was a persistence

49

in the misconception of the federal government as a sovereign power—aloof, remote, and magisterial—above and apart from people and their daily life. What had to be done was to bring government down into the world of work where it could see and serve the country's needs, correcting every injustice and evil inequality.

The fundamentals of what he was to call the New Deal were already clear in his mind, fruit of the reading and thinking that he had been doing since his affliction. As he saw it, a government that could not provide work for the strong and willing and that let the black shadow of insecurity rest on every home was not a government which could endure or should endure. In the new light that had come to him, he held to the belief that the welfare of the individual depended on the welfare of the whole; that prosperity began at the bottom, not the top; and that the march of progress was measured by the last man in the procession, not the first.

What he dreamed was a new order that would assure opportunity to youth and comfort and dignity to old age; an order outlawing the brutalities of greed; an order that would give life greater generosity and a larger measure of happiness; an order permitting expression of the best in man, not the basest, and under which wolfish hates would not be a necessary part of the struggle for existence.

As governor of New York, going about the state

1929, he had passed many an idle factory, and all of them he saw machinery packed in grease and covered with tarpaulin. Watchmen patrolled the buildings to guard against fire, and thousands of dollars were being spent to make sure that the machines would be as good as new when operations were resumed. Outside the gates of those factories, however, he found crowds of jobless men, huddled and miserable, and not one single cent was being spent to see that *they* were being kept as good as new against the day when they would be needed again.

"Every time I saw such sights," he said, "I asked myself where was the practicality in counting human flesh and blood less important in the scheme of things than pieces of metal."

Looking out over a country robbed of its courage and optimism, he saw a thousand things to be done. Great adventures in conservation and reclamation, not only with respect to land but equally with respect to human resources; whole cities to be rebuilt, ending the shame of slums; a far-reaching social security program; laws to curb greed and provide equality of opportunity; a real education for youth; music and art for the enrichment of life and the endowment of leisure with beauty and dignity; a Good Neighbor policy that would weld the Western Hemisphere into an invincible phalanx. Catching fire from his dreams of a new and greater America, he gave his consent to Jim Farley's tour of the states in search of support.

51

There are those, I know, who maintain that ⟨Frank⟩lin Roosevelt was always the consummate politicia⟨n⟩ rather than the sincere humanitarian. There is no question that he did play politics, oftentimes to the limit; but heaven help the President who doesn't. When it came to human needs, however, I doubt if there was ever any public man less political in his thought. As governor of New York, one of his first activities was to provide better care for the sick, the poor, and the insane, and along with the building of modern institutions he launched a comprehensive health program that won the admiration of every doctor.

Even when laboring under the burdens of the presidency, he gave his instant and sympathetic attention to anything connected with health and healing. The National Naval Medical Center at Bethesda, Maryland, for example, was my suggestion, but in everything else it was the President's creation. I brought it up at a time when his load was at the peak; but on hearing the nature of the project, he put everything aside. My first thought was merely a hospital, but he conceived it instantly as a center, not only caring for the Navy's sick and wounded but contributing to civil medicine by the maintenance of research laboratories and training schools. With his own hands he drew the sketches; and Paul Cret, the famous architect, together with the Navy's Admiral Ben Moreell, accepted them

and was guided by them. Out of their joint consultations came one of the finest examples of mass and height in the architectural world, from which men have gone all over the globe to wage victorious battle against disease.

No, I can never be made to believe that Franklin Roosevelt was anything but genuine in his whole-hearted humanitarianism, nor do I believe that the American people themselves ever entertained a doubt. Proof of it lies in the election returns of 1932, 1936, 1940, and 1944. Millions aren't fooled for twelve long years.

Back in the 1932 campaign the bare mention of Governor Roosevelt's name in connection with the presidency immediately stirred new discussions as to his physical condition, and the gossip spread that he could not possibly stand the strain of that high office. In 1930 life insurance companies had written policies on him in the amount of $560,000, all for the benefit of the Warm Springs Foundation, but even this did not stop malicious tongues.

In April 1931, therefore, when the attack was at its height, he met it head on by consenting to an examination by three eminent physicians. Dr. Samuel W. Lambert, diagnostician, Dr. Russell A. Hibbs, orthopedist, and Dr. Foster Kennedy, neurologist, were the ones chosen, and after going over him from head to foot, they rendered this report:

We have today examined Franklin D. Roosevelt. We find that his organs and functions are sound in all respects. There is no anemia. The chest is exceptionally well developed, and the spinal column is perfectly normal; all of its segments are in perfect alignment, and free from disease. He has neither pain nor ache at any time.

Ten years ago, Governor Roosevelt suffered an attack of acute infantile paralysis, the entire effect of which was expended on the muscles of his lower extremities. There has been progressive recovery of power in the legs since that date; this restoration continues and will continue. Governor Roosevelt can walk all necessary distances and can maintain a standing position without fatigue. We believe that his powers of endurance are such as to allow him to meet all demands of private or public life.

Thus armed against one phase of political attack, he announced his candidacy and launched his campaign.

CHAPTER V

WHITE HOUSE PHYSICIAN

O**N DUTY AT THE NAVAL HOSPITAL IN WASHINGTON** in 1932, I followed the campaign with intense interest and rejoiced in the outcome, although never dreaming that it would have any personal meaning. As Assistant Secretary of the Navy, Franklin Roosevelt had shown me certain kindnesses, but that was his generous way with junior officers; and while I held him in deep admiration, it was without thought of being remembered.

To be quite honest, I wasn't; for my appointment as White House physician came through Admiral Cary Grayson. There is no embarrassment in the confession, however, for the Admiral's friendship will ever mean as much to me as the honor that came through it. I first met him in 1917 when I came to Washington as an assistant surgeon in the Medical Corps of the Navy, having just quit my private practice in Oregon. He was then White House physician, but nothing could have been more considerate than his treatment of a young lieutenant—junior grade at that. After three years at sea I had the privilege of association with him again in Washington; and when I was assigned to the U. S. Naval Dispensary in 1925, he was my commanding officer.

A kinder, more thoughtful man, I never knew. Not once but scores of times Cary Grayson came to me with poor devils who stood in need of an operation, begging to know if I could do the necessary surgery outside and away from my regular duties. And always the hospital bills came out of his private purse. Small wonder that he was so loved.

Another round of sea duty took me away from Washington for several years, but 1931 found me back at the Naval Hospital, and with additional duties as an instructor in ophthalmology and otolaryngology in the Naval Medical School. At the time Admiral Grayson was deeply interested in the tropical-disease research of the Gorgas Memorial Institute, and our close relations were resumed. As one of Franklin Roosevelt's oldest and dearest friends, the Admiral became a White House intimate after the 1932 election, and thought of me when the President asked him about a physician.

My selection, of course, came as a complete surprise; and, while the honor lifted me sky-high, it also brought a sense of deep responsibility. What could an eye, ear, nose, and throat man possibly have to offer to a victim of infantile paralysis? Cary only laughed when I went to him with my fears, and told me to quit worrying. "The President," he said, "is as strong as a horse with the exception of a chronic sinus condition that makes him susceptible to colds. That's where you come in."

This made me feel better, for I did think I knew my specialty, what with years of practice and teaching, and many special postgraduate courses. Any comfort that I took from my training and experience soon vanished, however, when I began reading up on the background and nature of my new job. Civilian practitioners sit in their offices until called, but a White House physician may not wait until the President picks up a germ, runs a temperature, or breaks out in a rash. The job is to *keep* him well, to *guard* him against illness, and that entails daily observation and constant watchfulness. Since these visits must fit into the work day of the chief executive, if they are not to become an interruption and annoyance, it follows that the medicine man of the Great White Father must have the run of the place as a liked and trusted intimate, equally at home in parlor, bedroom, and bath.

Fortunately, a president has a free hand in the selection of his physician, for Congress has never manifested any concern for the health of the nation's head. To this day there is no permanent summer home to which he can retreat during Washington's torrid season, and it was not until 1937 that an inadequate air-cooling system was installed in the White House. Only the safety of the President has ever been made the subject of statutory enactment. The Treasury Department, back in the days before the F.B.I., was specifically instructed to guard him at all times, and men of the Secret Service have their regular posts at the White House. Every visitor runs the gantlet of their scrutiny.

The health of the chief executive, however, is his own private business. Through long-established custom it is the habit of presidents to select either an Army or a Navy doctor when the time comes for them to choose the medico who will look after their well-being. There are many good reasons for naming a member of the service. These men are officers as well as physicians, and being subject to the iron discipline of the armed services, they can be counted on to keep a close mouth about what they see and hear.

It is also the case that a civilian practitioner could not pick up at a moment's notice, dash here and there with the President, and find much of a private practice on his return. Nor should it be overlooked that the fees for a civilian doctor would have to come out of the chief executive's own pocket, a fairly heavy burden.

On account of the inescapable intimacy of the relationship, the selection is usually dictated by purely personal reasons. Is the President's medical adviser likable and companionable as well as a competent doctor? Will he fit into the household? Dr. Jonathan M. Foltz, the first regular White House physician, was a family friend of James Buchanan and had his own room in the White House. Colonel Robert M. O'Reilly came to Grover Cleveland's attention through their common love of fishing, and Dr. P. M. Rixey's tender care of Mrs. McKinley won the affectionate regard of the President. Learning that the big, dynamic Navy surgeon was a mighty hunter and a superb horseman, Theodore Roosevelt kept Dr. Rixey on as a companion rather than a physician.

William H. Taft changed to the Army, appointing Colonel A. M. Delaney, but also made much use of Cary Grayson, then a young officer in the Navy Medical Service who had been Dr. Rixey's aide during the Roosevelt administration. When he turned his office over to Woodrow Wilson, Mr. Taft placed his hand on Cary's shoulder and said, "Here's an excellent fellow I hope you'll get to know. He's a Virginian and a Democrat, but that's the only wrong thing about him." Dr. Grayson became an integral and beloved part of the Wilson household, and more than any other, in my opinion, was the man the President most trusted.

Dr. Charles B. Sawyer, a homeopath, was brought to Washington by President Harding. He was not only a close friend but had been Mrs. Harding's personal physician for many years. I still recall, and with much of the old bitterness, the howl that went up from the press when President Wilson promoted Cary Grayson to be rear admiral as a proper and deserved recognition for his fruitful service to three chief executives —Theodore Roosevelt, Taft, and Wilson. Not one word of criticism, however, was heard when President Harding gave Dr. Sawyer the rank of brigadier general.

President Coolidge swung back to the Army, choosing Major James F. Coupal to be the White House physician, but President Hoover returned to the Navy, selecting Captain Joel T. Boone. Neither doctor left behind any volume of comment, for both chief executives enjoyed good health throughout their terms. Such autobiographies as had been written, however, gave me ample food for apprehension.

Both Dr. Foltz and Dr. Rixey stressed the intensely personal nature of the relation between the White House physician and the President, and the latter, in particular, made it clear that some of his patients were pretty hard to handle. President McKinley spent all of his spare time at the bedside of his sick wife and could not be induced to take exercise of any kind. As a result, the assassin's bullet found him in such a run-down condition that he could offer little physical resistance.

Theodore Roosevelt, on the other hand, could not be kept from overdoing. The apostle of the Strenuous Life, he insisted on living it; and when not boxing, wrestling, fencing, or singlesticking, he careered over the landscape on a horse. There was the time, writes Dr. Rixey, when T. R. ordered Army officers to ride one hundred miles in a day by way of proving fitness, and then answered complaints from overweight generals by doing it himself.

Woodrow Wilson, despite Dr. Grayson's protests and entreaties, refused to stick to the regimen that had been laid down for him. More and more it became his habit to work late into the night, poring over state papers or else pounding out memoranda and speeches on his own ancient little typewriter. In Paris at the peace conference he could not be persuaded to rest, even after an attack of influenza, and came back in a sadly weakened condition. It was in stubborn disregard of Dr. Grayson's warnings that President Wilson went on the tragic tour of the country that ended in his collapse.

What if F. D. R. turned out to be stubborn and intractable? What if I did not fit in? What if I got on my patient's nerves? All of these fears persisted until my first official interview with the President. "Cary Grayson," he said, "told me that anybody can get along with you, so the success of our association seems to be up to me." There was not only heart-warming courtesy, consideration, and warm friendliness, but better than all, a clear understanding both of his own case and the task that lay ahead. He had watched Woodrow Wilson, his beloved chief, wear himself out, and knew exactly what he was tackling.

It is rare indeed for anyone to consider the presidency in the light of a *job*, but a conscientious chief executive is called upon for more downright drudgery than any other official in the world. The position still runs exactly along the lines laid down in 1787, when the population of the entire country totaled less than the 1946 census of New York City. As a result, the duties are a queer, impossible jumble of tremendous problems and absurd clerical routine calculated to break the strongest.

Harold Smith, Director of the Budget, recently pointed out some of the more glaring instances. To mention only a few, the President must issue and sign regulations governing prize fights in the Panama Canal Zone; approve higher salaries for Public Health Service doctors who come in contact with lepers; specify the exact size of officers' insignia and the way to wear them; personally authorize and sign every proclamation for this or that "national day"; approve the site and construction of veterans' hospitals and the transfer of real and personal property between the Tennessee Valley Authority and other government agencies.

It is also the case that he must sign and issue formal executive orders for such trivial matters as these: requiring ships in transit in the Panama Canal during the noon hour to supply luncheon to Canal employees on board; changing the name of a customs port of entry in Oregon from Marshfield to Coos Bay; officially designating as a prize of war a captured German motor vessel. As a further aid to writer's cramp, he must sign thousands of commissions in connection with appointments. Others can delegate these purely clerical tasks, but not the President of the United States.

Most crushing burden of all, as Mr. Smith makes clear in painful detail, is imposed by "the ancient, moss-grown system of private bills." After Congress has solemnly considered the justice of a claim for a hundred dollars, filed by a Texas farmer whose watermelons were stolen by soldiers, the President must also give the matter his time and thought before signing the bill. Or maybe it is a case involving $23.50 for damage done to a private car by an Army truck. Absurdly trivial, but only the chief executive has the power to make final settlement.

President Roosevelt, in no doubt as to the load that he must carry, agreed with me on the necessity of a fixed routine that would order every hour of the day with machine-like exactitude. Certain hours for work, certain hours for sleep, regular exercise, careful attention to diet, and some sort of vacation every three months.

In accordance with the routine decided on, I parked my car before the White House every morning around 8:30 and went to the President's bedroom for a look-see. Neither the thermometer nor stethoscope was produced, there was no request for a look at the tongue or a feel of the pulse, and only rarely was a direct question ever asked. Finding myself a comfortable chair, I sat a bit while breakfast was being eaten or the morning papers looked over.

A close but seemingly casual watch told all I wanted to know. The things that interested me most were the President's color, the tone of his voice, the tilt of his chin, and the way he tackled his orange juice, cereal, and eggs. Satisfied on these points, I went away and devoted the rest of the day to my own affairs. Not inconsiderable, if I may be pardoned for saying so, for at the time I was head of the eye, ear, nose, and throat department in the Naval Hospital, and also teaching at the Naval Medical Center. After 1938, when the President was generous enough to make me surgeon general of the Navy with the rank of rear admiral, my duties became even more exacting. At the height of the war the Medical Department of the Navy, which came under my direction, was made up of 175,000 doctors, dentists, nurses, and hospital corpsmen, 52 general hospitals, and 278 mobile hospitals all over the world, running from 25 beds to 1,500.

In the afternoon, promptly at 5:30, I made a second call, parking outside the executive offices. This time my approach was more direct, for I was there to see that the President shut up shop and trundled over to the White House, either for a swim in the pool or a rest before dinner. I also took a shrewd peek at his work basket to make sure that the pile of documents and memoranda was not so large that it meant a long stretch of night work. On his trips, both at home and abroad, I usually gave the President the "once over" at bedtime.

What helped me and my job immeasurably was the swimming pool, fifty feet long, fifteen feet wide, and nine feet deep at one end. Curiously enough, the President owed it to the New York *Daily News,* a paper that became his bitterest critic in later years. Knowing that there had been a pool in Albany, Joseph Patterson asked permission to raise funds by popular subscription to install one in the White House. The President consented gladly, and Congress enacted the necessary legislation.

A dozen or more newspapers throughout the country joined in the campaign, and the pennies, nickels, and dimes of school children were the principal contributions. Within a week the needed sum was raised, and the *Daily News* sent an architect to Washington for consultation with the President. The space selected had previously been taken up by the White House laundry. According to Steve Early, manufacturers and supply houses had a part in the gift. The tiles were donated, likewise the sunray lamps in the side walls and the necessary apparatus for purifying and heating the water by thermostatic control. As Steve rather caustically commented in a recent note to me, "It is the only health builder that any President of the United States will find in the White House. All else that I know anything about is decidedly destructive."

Because of his love for the water, it was easy to persuade the President that the day's work must stop at 5:30, giving him an hour in the pool before dinner.

This time was the happiest in the whole day, for his mighty back muscles made him the equal of any, and he loved to duck and wrestle and race. Having mastered a modified Australian crawl, he preferred it, but I made him cut out underwater swimming because of his tendency to sinus infections.

Always, as at Warm Springs, a part of the time was devoted to the muscle-stretching exercises that he had worked out for himself. The patient persistence with which he tugged, turned, and twisted was a lesson in self-discipline. After the swim the President took his place on the rubbing table, where George Fox would give him a thorough massage. Here, by the way, was one to whom four presidents owed much. Starting as an enlisted man in the Hospital Corps of the Navy, Fox earned, by virtue of his special training in physical therapy, an assignment to the White House during Woodrow Wilson's illness. Admiral Grayson brought him back from sea duty to look after President Coolidge, and he was permanently attached to the White House during Mr. Hoover's term. One of my first acts was to make sure that George would be kept at my side, and I can never speak too warmly of his invaluable services. The President himself was no less appreciative, and Fox's ultimate lift to the rank of commander was a just reward for missed promotions due to the peculiar form of duty that was his lot for so many years.

Physical examinations, of course, constituted a part

66

of the regular routine. Once a year we went over the President from head to foot, and special checkups were frequent. The kidneys were checked every month, and extra blood pictures were taken on some occasions for special reasons. Now and then famous consultants were called in, but as a usual thing I relied on our Navy specialists. Not only did I consider them to be as good as the best, but there was the advantage that journeys to the Medical Center could be made without exciting comment. At no time did I have any quarrel with the co-operation of the Washington correspondents, but a visit of the President to the Mayos or Johns Hopkins, even for a routine checkup, was bound to have been played up as big news.

I had not been White House physician for any length of time before I discovered that I did not have just one patient but a *family*. Not a small one either, for aside from the secretariat and the workers in the executive offices, there were the Secret Service men, the White House police, the ushers, the domestic help, and so on. I did not have the direct care of them, to be sure, but it was necessary to ride herd on them very closely, for there was the risk that their ailments might be communicated to the President.

From the first, therefore, I established a close relationship with all of them, stressing the importance of consulting me if occasion demanded, and training them as helpers. Particularly the kitchen staff, for it was vitally necessary that a watch be kept on the

67

water, the milk, and the condition of the greenstuffs that came in from all sources.

Sinus flare-ups were my chief worry, for the President's one susceptibility was to colds. Guarding him from them was far from easy, for the White House is not a private home by any means. The delegations that stream in and stream out do not bring their own cubic feet of air space, nor is it possible to search them for germs and splash them with disinfectants. Everybody about the White House, therefore, was pressed into service. If it happened that a caller presented himself with a drippy nose, Pa Watson invariably found an excuse for postponing the appointment. Missy Le Hand and Grace Tully could detect a draft at one hundred paces, and even the ushers became experts on ventilation. After a press conference, or some other mob scene, the executive offices were thoroughly aired.

Louis McHenry Howe, of course, was one of my main dependences until the day of his untimely death, for with the intimacy of a years-long friendship he could buck the Boss's Dutch stubbornness when occasion required. Immediately following my initial conference with the President, Louie summoned me to his office, and after a searching examination was pleased to approve the daily schedule decided on. "O.K.," he barked, "I'll see that Franklin holds to it." And he did help in many ways. Louie was the only one of the official family who called the President

"Franklin." It was "Mr. President" or "the Boss" for the rest of us.

Naval aides, because of the President's love of the service, were important members of the "family," although the demands of sea duty necessitated many changes. First came Rear Admiral Walter N. Vernou and then this succession; Rear Admiral Wilson Brown, Captain Paul Bastedo, Captain Daniel J. Callaghan, Rear Admiral John Beardall, and Captain John Mc-Crea, then Admiral Brown again. The President leaned on each of them and followed all with affectionate interest when they sailed away. I will never forget his grief when the news came that Admiral Dan Callaghan had been blown to pieces while fighting his flagship, the *San Francisco*, in the epic naval battle off Savo Island.

General Edwin Watson, a gallant soldier with a distinguished record in the First World War, joined the President's staff as military aide in 1933 and added the duties of appointment secretary after Marvin McIntyre's death. His gay good humor was a joy to the Boss, but for all his carefree joviality he had a keen judgment and the gift of crisp decision. Here again was one who never spared himself in the President's service, and his collapse on the return trip from Yalta stemmed largely from the mental and physical strain of twelve White House years.

Rudolph Forster, chief clerk, entered the government service during McKinley's administration, and

F.D.R. came to trust him just as had Theodore Roosevelt, Taft, Wilson, Harding, Coolidge, and Hoover. Maurice Latta, his assistant and his successor when Rudolph's heart could no longer carry the load, was another old-timer; and the two made a team that handled the executive office's mass of detail with rare ability. William Hassett, Steve Early's assistant and often his substitute, also looked after a good deal of the President's personal correspondence, and attained amazing skill in acquiring F.D.R.'s style and intimate touch.

Marguerite Le Hand was more the guide, philosopher, and friend than just a confidential secretary. She had been with the Roosevelts since the early twenties and by reason of loyalty, brains, and high character had become an integral and invaluable part of their lives. She knew F.D.R. almost as well as he knew himself; and when I ran up against his Dutch side, it was always to Missy that I appealed, confident that she would bring him around. An attack of rheumatic fever in 1926 left her with a heart condition, but as in the case of Louie Howe, Marvin McIntyre, and Pa Watson, she could not be induced to slow down, and her untimely passing left a gap that could not be filled.

Gay, able, charming Grace Tully was Number Two on the personal staff, and Dorothy Brady Number Three. Roberta Barrows, first the right hand of Marvin McIntyre and then inherited by General Watson, also helped out on the President's work and accompanied us on many trips. These three completed the competent and devoted group that gave the President love and loyalty as well as brilliant service. That he managed to stand the strain as well as he did was due to their watchfulness and unfailing efforts to lighten his load.

Naturally, however, my best helper was Mrs. Roosevelt. It was not only her gift for administration that made the White House a smooth-running machine, but the kindness and thoughtfulness that endeared her to every member of the household. As an old doorman, who had seen presidents and their wives come and go, once said to me, "The Madam knows how to treat people. There's not one of us that wouldn't do anything for her." Throughout our whole association there was never a suggestion of mine, regarding the President's care, that was not put into instant and effective action.

More than this, she took much of her husband's load off of his shoulders, so that he could live within his own reserve. From the first she was pressed into service as a sort of woman-of-all-work, pinch hitting for the President at various gatherings, making surveys, rendering reports, and maintaining the close touch with people that he demanded. Much has been written of her tireless energy, and it is all true. There were many times when I knew her to be desperately fatigued, but only once did we manage to call a halt, and that was for forty-eight hours when she had a severe attack of influenza.

Notwithstanding her broad national interests—slum clearance, better housing, higher living standards, etc. —she never lost the intimate personal touch. She will not thank me for mentioning it, but I happen to know that in addition to contributions to charitable organizations, she spent a large percentage of her income in direct help to individuals. Before every journey she always asked me about the location of service hospitals and if I thought a visit to them would be of help. The hours she spent with wounded men, both in this country and the Solomons and Hawaii, had healing value, and no less appreciated were the hundreds of messages that she brought back to families and transmitted with unfailing care.

Looking back over the years, I realize how much I owe to Mrs. Roosevelt. The manner in which the President carried his burdens through three terms, and on into the fourth, was largely due to her unfailing co-operation and intelligent assistance.

CHAPTER VI

F.D.R. AS A PATIENT

WITH DAILY CONTACT BRINGING A BETTER UNDER-
standing both of my charge and the job, I began
to shed my early doubts and apprehensions. As Cary
Grayson had predicted, I found the President a "rugged individual" and mighty close to being as strong
as a horse. The morning and afternoon calls were more
social than professional, and it came to be quite a joke
that I went with him on his trips "just for the ride."
He himself liked to refer to me as a "hitchhiker."

In common with others of the White House circle,
I lost sight of his infirmity, even ignoring the sharp
click of the steel braces when he snapped them into
place. With his usual patience he had worked out a
method of handling them that minimized their awk-
wardness. Not a simple business either, for Jimmy
Roosevelt, young and husky, failed to master the
technique after repeated trials. On the flat he could
do fairly well but tumbled all over himself trying to
climb stairs.

These braces, skillfully built, carried the President's

73

weight without mishap except on the occasion of his acceptance speech in 1936. A crowd of more than 100,000 jammed the Philadelphia stadium as he entered from the rear of a jam-packed stadium. Bands played and floodlights gleamed on his smiling face. Waving his hands in greeting, he advanced a few steps to the speaker's platform and then, as it seemed to the crowd, was shut out from view by a rush of officials.

What actually happened was that a bolt in one of his braces became unlocked, throwing the President completely off balance and scattering the pages of his typewritten speech as they flew from his hand. Ever watchful Gus Gennerich caught him before he could fall, and Jim Farley, Homer Cummings, and several other tall men quickly formed a screen that shut off the gaze of the crowd. As Jimmy Roosevelt supported his father, Gus relocked the brace.

The manuscript was picked up without any effort to put the sheets in their proper place; and a moment later the President mounted the rostrum, smiling broadly as if he had merely stopped to greet some friends. The people in the audience never knew what happened, and only the newspapermen noticed as he paused at intervals to reshuffle the misplaced pages of his speech.

Because of the President's nervous energy and his refusal to be regarded as a cripple, the possibility of a fall never ceased to be a worry, and this gave importance to the selection of personal attendants. Fortunately, Gus Gennerich had been with him since the Albany days. A police sergeant in New York at the time of his employment as bodyguard, along with the strength of a bull he had deft, gentle hands. When the President stood or walked, Gus could support him without seeming to do so, and had a fine technique in helping him to board trains and move about in small boats. His sudden death due to a coronary thrombosis, while he was on one of our South American cruises, was both a shock and a loss. Gus was followed by Tommy Qualters, a member of the New York State Police, another competent, intelligent, and loyal aide. Tommy left to put on a uniform and saw active service in the European theater.

Hating to be "fussed over," the President developed remarkable skill in getting in and out of bed by himself, and also took a lot of pride in putting on and taking off his clothes. McDuffie, his first valet, and then Arthur Prettyman, both devoted and intelligent colored men, watched like hawks even while they humored him. More than that, they became very good diagnosticians and reported to me whenever they thought that the President had had a bad night, or if he seemed to be off his food.

Temperate in all things, the President ate and drank in strict accordance with the rules we had agreed on. Not until the war years, when he lost appetite, was there any trouble about diet. An unvarying breakfast dish was ham or bacon and eggs, and I had more than

75

a suspicion that this was because Fala also liked that menu. He relished fish and game but avoided sweets out of a dread of putting on weight. On motor trips or picnics he never failed to insist on frankfurters and beer, and I shall always remember his delight in acquainting King George and Queen Elizabeth with "hot dogs" on the occasion of their visit to Hyde Park.

As a usual thing, he took either a Martini or a whisky sour before dinner, chiefly the latter drink because he fancied himself as a mixer. Frequently, however, he would cut out alcohol for weeks at a time. Cigarettes were his weakness, despite the nasal irritations produced, and the best I could do was to get him to cut down on them during sinus attacks. His nights offered no problem, for he had trained himself to go to sleep within five minutes after turning out the light. Until the war no worry was ever carried to bed.

The President's disposition, in fact, was my most effective aid and greatest comfort. A sanguine temperament, almost adolescent in its buoyancy, kept him from brooding and guarded against those alternations of mood that tear at the nerves. Like everyone else, he had his angers and resentments, but they were never permitted to fester. Nor was he unduly elated over political victories or unduly depressed by setbacks.

A lot has been surmised, and a good deal said and written, about the aftereffects of polio on the nervous system. During the days when New Deal policies were exciting a large part of the population to wrathful

76

outbursts, nothing was more common than the charge that the President's affliction had left him "emotionally unstable" and very much less than well balanced. I have not been able to discover that polio specialists hold any such belief, and my association with the President certainly disproved it in every particular. More than any other person I have ever met, and I say this deliberately, he had equanimity, poise, and a serenity of temper that kept him on the most even of keels.

Matters of great moment, whether issues or events, were faced with unruffled calm. In the days that followed Pearl Harbor, for example, he was by far and away the least emotional of all those who gathered in the White House for consultation. Maybe there was an inner excitement, but if so it was translated into cool and effective action. What helped, of course, was his habit of looking ahead, so that very few things ever took him by surprise.

No president was ever more bitterly attacked, and yet I think that the White House correspondents will bear me out when I say that he never resented any blow that landed above the belt. What did anger him was unfair fighting, and his irritation was invariably stirred by the mean and little. Being "nibbled to death by ducks" was the way he phrased it. By his own confession a certain type of opposition always made him want to "lash out."

"Criticism," he explained, "unless constructive, is

77

nothing but abuse. They attack what I have done, but never once do they say what they would have done or would do. To answer attempts to end child labor, wipe out slums, and better living conditions by yelling that it is the opening wedge for a dictatorship that will destroy free speech, free press, free assemblage, and abolish trial by jury, *isn't* criticism in any honest sense of the word, but just plain, downright sabotage."

In the beginning of our association I had urged rest periods, but I soon discovered that what refreshed him most was not a discontinuance of activity but change of pace. His stamp collection was easily his favorite relaxation from strain. He had started the hobby as a boy of eight and held to it throughout his life. A half hour before his death, in fact, he had telephoned Postmaster General Frank Walker with regard to buying the first stamp of a new issue to commemorate the United Nations conference in San Francisco.

Contrary to press reports, his collection was not the most valuable in the world. Far from it. Up to the time that he entered the White House, he was known in the trade as a careful, even frugal, buyer, ten dollars being about as high as he liked to go. The collection, when valued by an expert for auction purposes, was appraised at $80,000, and that it brought a much larger amount was due to sentiment. Roosevelt enthusiasts from South America, for example, bought many stamps at ten times the estimated price.

I think it safe to say that there was not a day, even

during the war years, when he did not give half an hour to his stamps. Usually after he had retired and just before turning out the lamp. On every one of his journeys abroad he carried several albums, even if it meant cutting down on his personal effects. At Yalta, I remember particularly, he found his greatest relief from fatigue by working away at his albums at the end of each exhausting day.

Anything connected with stamps excited his eager interest. During his administrations 225 new designs were issued by the Post Office, and each of them had to receive his personal approval, not only the sketches but also the die proofs and color proofs. He himself drew the sketches for the Byrd Antarctic stamp and the Mother's Day stamp. A hobby, of course; but someday a treatise is going to be written on the therapeutic value of hobbies.

At the outset I also learned the uselessness of trying to cut down on his list of daily visitors. Never at any time one disposed to solitude or reticence but one of the most companionable men that ever lived, the President loved the give-and-take of conversation. The trouble was, as with every vivid personality, he gave more than he took. His talk was no mere adventure in anecdotes but a broad sweep, enriching and illuminating everything that it touched.

People, however, were as necessary to him as meat and drink, and until our entry into the war no president ever kept a wider open door. First Marvin Mc-

Intyre and then Pa Watson wore themselves out trying to cut down on the daily list of visitors, not to mention the job of getting them out after they got in. And always it was F.D.R. who protracted the interviews, his interest caught by something that had been said.

A story that Ray Moley loved to tell was about two nuts who showed up at Warm Springs just before the first inauguration, demanding to see the President-elect. Their talk was wild and violent, and poor Mac was alarmed to the point of calling in armed guards. F.D.R., hearing the discussion, had them admitted; and the three had quite a talk over some sort of "magic money" scheme. The pair left in high feather, and F.D.R. justified the interview by saying that "they *might* have had something. You never can tell."

Try as I might, I could not keep him from crowding his days. One thing against which I protested most strenuously was the way that many of his appointees ran to him with their problems. Instead of giving these "leaners" the boot the President encouraged them in the habit. His enemies, of course, charged that his egotism made him unwilling to delegate authority; but this was not the case at all. He loved to know everything that was going on and delighted to have a finger in every pie. Not until the war years, when time was the essence, could I persuade him to bar officials who wanted to dump their troubles on his shoulders.

At first I was also disposed to counsel against travel, but quit when I found that it was helpful rather than

80

hurtful. He slept in a berth even better than in his bed at the White House; change of scene and contact with people refreshed and invigorated instead of tiring him. Curiously enough, when he was out of doors away from walls, he seemed impervious to weather changes, enduring extremes of heat and cold and unaffected by exposure. For example, there was a trip in 1939 when we fished the waters in and around Newfoundland. A thunderstorm caught us on the Humber River, far up in the mountains, and when we got back to the ship, every member of the party was chilled and exhausted except the President. He razzed us as a bunch of mollycoddles, and the best I could do was to make him take a steaming hot bath.

Another of my early fears was press conferences. With two hundred sharp minds pelting him with questions and the danger of an unguarded word, they took a lot out of him, and I wanted the number cut down. The President, however, insisted that the values outweighed the risks, and made the point that much of Woodrow Wilson's trouble came from his failure to establish close relations with the Washington correspondents.

"W. W.," he said, "had a horror of what he called conjectural journalism. He felt that newspapermen were not interested in what *had* happened but only in what *might* happen. As he expressed it, their idea of news was the satisfaction of curiosity. Increasingly irritated, he quit holding press conferences and excited

81

a hostility that endured. I don't intend to make that mistake. Moreover," and he smiled broadly, "it happens that I *like* them. The clash of wits, the continual swordplay, is a lot of fun."

It is not true that the President, down in his heart, resented the fourth estate. The White House correspondents without exception were held in a very real affection; and, while F.D.R. often "dished it out," he also "took it." He made a sharp distinction, however, between newspapermen and columnists, regarding the latter as "excrescences." News, he insisted, was not their interest, but the gossip obtained by "keyhole" methods and from violations of confidence by unethical officials, either to win the columnist's favor or to satisfy a grudge.

Despite our bargain about regular vacations, I doubt, however, if he would have kept the agreement except for his love of the water and fishing. Not even Izaak Walton was ever more the Compleat Angler. After a day of battle with deep-sea big fellows, he would turn to me with a wheedling grin and say, "We've got another hour, so what about a bit of bottom fishing?"

The yacht *Potomac* was seaworthy enough for cruises in protected waters, such as the Bahamas, and you could fairly see the cares dropping off his shoulders as he went aboard. Then there were the voyages into the Caribbean and Pacific, made in connection with inspection tours or official visits. Days of fishing were always worked in, and the cruises also afforded opportunity for the exploration that he loved. As good a geographer as any navy man, he outstripped all of us when it came to history. The only time I ever stumped him was about the John Day River in my own home state of Oregon. He insisted that there wasn't any such stream, and it took a map to convince him.

In old Panama he made Sir Henry Morgan live again by his colorful account of sea battles and the pillage of cities; on Jefferson Island he had us wheel him over the crumbling fort built in 1846, and pointed out the cell of Dr. Samuel Mudd, that unhappy surgeon who had had the misfortune to attend John Wilkes Booth; in the San Blas country he described the life of the Indians as it had been lived for five hundred years; in the Galapagos he searched for the grave of the young American officer who lost his life in a duel when Commodore Porter, U.S.N., landed on the islands in 1813; always, when off Cocos Island, he bemoaned the lack of time that kept him from hunting for the treasure supposedly buried there after the sack of Lima.

These sea trips, of course, came to an end with Pearl Harbor, for there was the danger of German submarines offshore. This brought up the question of how to provide the President with the necessary vacation periods, especially during the debilitating heat of Washington summers. The problem was finally solved by the Government's acquisition of some acreage on Cotoctin Mountain, about thirty miles to the northwest. Simple but suitable accommodations were built, and because of the secrecy imposed for security reasons, F.D.R. named the hideaway Shangri-La.

Although liking the quiet mountain retreat, the President missed his sea trips and kept up his insistence that danger from German submarines was more fancied than real. Physical fear was left out of his make-up, and this made Colonel Starling's job very difficult at times. Before a trip the Colonel and his men went over the proposed routes in every city, oftentimes changing the line of march and arranging hotel accommodations in such manner as to provide for the most careful watch. The President never liked this close and ceaseless espionage, and it was not at all uncommon for him to kick over the traces.

In 1934, as an illustration, we started on a trip that carried us to Haiti, Columbia, the Panama Canal, Hawaii, and back to the Pacific Northwest. When we were three days out of Portland, a message came through that told of the discovery of a plot against his life. Only a year before, in Miami, Mayor Cermak had died of a bullet meant for the President-elect, and this added to our anxiety and alarm. Colonel Starling voiced the opinion of the whole party when he urged the cancellation of the Portland visit and a return to Washington.

"No," said the President. "That's absurd. Every public appearance of a chief executive entails an ele-

84

ment of risk; but do you want me to become a prisoner in the White House, more and more apprehensive until I'm afraid to go near a window? If anyone wants to kill me, there is no possible way to prevent him. About all that can be done is to guard against a second shot. I will ride through the streets of Portland as planned and announced, and the best you can do, Colonel, is to take every reasonable precaution." All Oregon turned out, and the jam of people blocked our cars at many points; but, while the rest of us rode with our hearts in our throats, I couldn't see the slightest sign of strain in F.D.R.

Another clash of wills came in 1937. Following the inaugural address, the Secret Service insisted that the President ride back to the White House in a closed car, pointing out that Washington was filled with thousands of strangers. As a driving rain was coming down in sheets, I joined in the request; but he would not listen to us. "The people," he said, "have been standing in the storm for hours, waiting to see me. I can do as much."

This utter lack of nervous apprehensions was never more clearly shown than on our South American tour in 1936. Shortly before our arrival in Uruguay some fanatic had stepped up to the president of the country and pumped a bullet into him that just missed the heart. When we reached Montevideo, the convalescing chief executive, quite naturally, did not want his American visitor to drive through the streets in an

85

open car. The Secret Service boys backed him up, but F.D.R. would not hear of any change in plans.

"Nonsense!" he laughed. "I can't see where I run any risk. *You*," giving the Uruguayan a poke in the ribs, "are the president they're out to get."

Colonel Starling always lamented that I had much the easier job, claiming that the one danger the White House physician had to guard against was colds. I thought so myself until the war years.

CHAPTER VII

"KITCHEN CABINETS"

NOTHING WAS EVER MORE ABSURD THAN THE CHARGE that one man, two men, or any set of men had a lien on the President's private ear. There were intimates whose judgment he respected, and in whose fidelity he had full faith, but by no means did he keep his eggs in a "kitchen cabinet" basket. Senators and congressmen of all parties, labor leaders, college professors, professional men, businessmen, and plain, simple everyday folks streamed in and out of his office, and through them he kept a finger on the public pulse. As he once said to me, "I entered the White House with the fixed determination that there would be no closed doors and no closed minds."

On his trips through the country he talked with the engineer who drove the train, the porter who made up his berth, and the local dignitaries who piled on board at every stop. If in a car, he would halt for a word with a farmer in the field; in towns with the butcher, the baker, and the candlestick maker; and in factories with the workers. Not just casual chats but inquiries calculated to develop what they were thinking and how they thought things were going.

Once stored, every piece of information was held fast by his retentive memory. Now and then, when a statement would be made about something that had gone before, he would give the original conversation verbatim, and a check would show that he had not misplaced a word. In 1936, for example, we had a rather large incident of polio in Georgia, the Carolinas, and even around Washington; and one of the measures taken was an attempt to seal off an area in the upper part of the nasal cavity so as to prevent the polio virus from entering the brain. I told the President about it in considerable detail; and a year later, when the epidemic broke out again in a different section, he repeated the conversation word for word, medical phraseology and all. Unhappily, when he asked me how the experiment had turned out, I was forced to tell him that it had proved of little avail in reducing infections.

Many of the President's policies, supposedly conceived by others, were purely his own. Out of his inspection trips through the Dust Bowl in the drought years of 1934–35 came his decision to build great dams, useful alike for power, irrigation, and flood control; his conception of the Civilian Conservation Corps both as a reforestation agency and a body and character builder for America's youth; tree belts for the arid areas of the West; and the Soil Conservation

88

Service that has done such a tremendous job in combating erosion. The story of a farmer who had been ruined by a bank failure, told to him at Warm Springs, had much to do with the law insuring bank deposits; and the Securities and Exchange Commission came into being out of his own personal knowledge of "blue sky" swindles.

It is my guess, based on observation, that Louie Howe was the nearest to a counselor in the word's true sense. Aside from the love that the President bore him by reason of the long years of devoted companionship, Louie had a keen appreciation of political values and an almost uncanny ability to foresee trends. Until his breakdown and death in 1935, he was the President's alter ego, never hesitating to object, dissent, and resist when he thought the course unwise.

Stephen Early and Marvin McIntyre, also pre-White House friends and associates, were others whose forthrightness disproved the sneer that the President wanted only "yes men" about him. Steve was unerring in his judgment of public opinion, and I will always regret that he was not at F.D.R.'s side at Casablanca and Teheran. Mac had the trying job of handling appointments, singling the few out of the many who clamored to have a word with the President. Gay and companionable, never troubling to take care of himself, he finally cracked under the strain.

What the President wanted most, in my opinion, was information on which to base intelligent findings.

As a consequence, most of his so-called advisers were really research men or authorities on the subject that happened to be his interest at the time. Once in possession of every fact in the case, he withdrew to commence the business of consideration, comparison, and assessment, and then emerged with a decision.

The famous "Brain Trust" had its origin in the 1932 campaign when Louie Howe saw the need of technical handy men to collect data for the preparation of speeches. Raymond Moley, then professor of public law at Columbia and with a rich background of practical as well as academic experience, was the first selection. Frank Walker was both a close friend and adviser throughout all the White House years. Others soon added were Rexford Guy Tugwell, Adolph Berle, Jr., General Hugh Johnson, Sam Rosenman, and various helpers. They collected facts and figures, made the first drafts of speeches, and prepared group memoranda on policies.

After the election many were placed in government posts and continued to constitute an intimate circle, valued for their companionship as well as specialized abilities. Felix Frankfurter came specifically into the picture in connection with the Securities and Exchange Act and stayed even after his elevation to the Supreme Court bench. Quite a few of his "boys" followed him, notably Tommy Corcoran, James M. Landis, Dean Acheson, and Francis Biddle. Corcoran, teaming up with Ben V. Cohen, was exceedingly useful by reason of his skill at whipping bills into shape, and "the Cork's" accordion and Irish songs livened many a White House evening.

Ray Moley, I think, was the one whose counsel was most valued and heeded by the President, for along with his fine mind he had a gift of cool detachment and logical reasoning that offset F.D.R.'s leaping enthusiasms. His loss was keenly felt when he resigned as Assistant Secretary of State and returned to the more congenial atmosphere of Columbia University. There was never any break, either with Secretary Hull or the President. Ray had never wanted a government post, and when he finally yielded to the President's direct request, it was with the understanding that he would be permitted to leave at an early date. He continued to be a White House visitor, always warmly welcomed, and it was not until 1936 that a widening divergence of views on certain New Deal policies led to a lessening of the old intimate association.

After the death of Louie Howe and Ray Moley's flight from Washington, Felix Frankfurter and his group were closest to the President; but when war clouds gathered in 1940, two men took precedence over all others. As a senator "Jimmie" Byrnes had been the stalwart champion of every New Deal measure, invaluable by reason of his parliamentary skill; and it was out of his appreciation of the South Carolinian's liberalism and ability that the President appointed him to the Supreme Court in 1941. And in 1942, when things were in a good deal of a mess, it was to Justice Byrnes that the President turned, asking him to quit the bench and take over as Director of Economic Stabilization. One year later, with his administrative genius fully proved, the President lifted Jimmie up to be Director of War Mobilization. Stepping down from his seat on the highest court of the land must have been a sacrifice, but never once was a moan heard to come out of him.

Harry Hopkins was the other *fidus Achates* entering the White House as a member of the family circle, and remaining inseparable until the end. Few men, I think it safe to say, were ever more bitterly attacked. As head of the WPA he had been called the most reckless waster of the taxpayers' money in all history, and the whole country roared with indignation when he was alleged to have said, "Spend and spend; tax and tax; elect and elect." As special assistant to the President, the opposition assailed him as a Rasputin and shuddered at the thought of such a man sleeping in Abraham Lincoln's bed.

I am without special knowledge to attempt any evaluation of Harry Hopkins' administration of the WPA or his brief service as Secretary of Commerce, but I can speak with some authority about his White House years. He gave to Franklin Roosevelt the man a companionship that comforted many lonely hours; and he gave to Franklin Roosevelt the President a single-minded devotion that took no thought of self.

As I sized it up, Harry was not the *mind* of the President but his eyes and ears, his trouble shooter, man-of-all-work, and even errand boy, although every errand had high importance. From bureaus and departments he gathered their needs, and digested them for the President's decision, saving him the burden of extended conferences. He broke bottlenecks; ferreted out the cause of interdepartmental conflicts, duplications, and overlapping; and acted as an effective liaison between the White House and the Army and the Navy. General Marshall, Admiral King, and others of the high command have borne witness to his usefulness.

It was not as an independent agent that he conferred with Prime Minister Churchill, Marshal Stalin, and the heads of governments, but as the *messenger* of the President, able to present his views without change or coloring, and receiving in return their views for transmission to the White House. His utter lack of vanity made him invaluable as a roving envoy, for it saved him from the temptation to intrude his own opinions and complicate situations by the assertion of his own personality.

All of the people in the President's official family came under my eye and care, and of the number none was ever more disregardful of his physical well-being than Harry Hopkins. Reckless as to diet, and hating to go to bed, he always drove himself at top speed. Even when in pain from stomach ulcers, he said nothing about them until his perceptible loss of weight made me demand an examination. An operation was plainly indicated, and in 1937 I sent him to the Mayo-Clinic where a full two-thirds of his stomach was removed. The result was a very definite improvement, but finding a proper diet proved difficult, and in 1938 intestinal upsets began to be frequent.

The symptoms were markedly similar to those of sprue, a food-deficiency disease fairly common in tropical countries, and I called in Rear Admiral Stitt, formerly surgeon general of the Navy, along with other specialists. Study developed that Harry's trouble came from an imbalance of proteins in the blood stream, and the use of blood substitutes soon helped him to a better assimilation of his food. Keeping him to a routine, however, proved an impossibility. At the Casablanca conference he would not take time for treatments, and by reason of flying here and there on various missions for the President, came to the date of the Teheran meeting in wretched shape. The sea voyage on the *Iowa* gave me an opportunity to fill him full of plasma and regulate his diet, but Harry kicked over the traces at the conferences in Egypt and Iran, working himself to a shadow.

By March 1944 his condition was so alarming that drastic operative procedures were deemed necessary to give him better absorption from his gastrointestinal tract. While this was successful from the surgical standpoint, it was not until July that he began to show steady gains. As always, any improvement made him impatient of treatment; so when the time came for the Yalta journey, he refused to sail with the President on the *Quincy*, flying to London, Paris, and Rome for preconference discussions. What he accomplished was important, but at a heavy price, for when he joined our party in Malta, Harry was completely exhausted. At Yalta, as a consequence, he spent most of the time in bed, and there were times when I did not think we would bring him back alive.

A long rest was imperative, but Harry could not be induced to put down any part of his load, and all that we could do was to rely on plasma and liver extract. The President's death was a terrible blow, and before he had a chance to recover from the shock, Mr. Truman asked him to go to Moscow. Marshal Stalin was showing no disposition whatsoever to keep his agreements with respect to Poland, and there was the hope that Harry could persuade him to a more co-operative course of action. He was careful to avoid me as he made ready for the trip, doubtless fearful that I would forbid it, and flew off without the slightest provision for medical care. There is no question in my mind that the strain of the journey led to his death in January 1946.

Admiral William D. Leahy's close association with the President began when he was Chief of Naval Operations, and continued without a break. His inclusion in the White House inner circle came about in a manner that is illustrative of F.D.R.'s capacity for

95

quick decisions. We were reviewing the fleet in 1939, the year of the Admiral's retirement, and on an evening when our party lay off Puerto Rico, the President started a discussion as to the future of the territory. He had improved conditions in the Virgin Islands by developing the rum industry; but Puerto Rico, with a population far in excess of its resources, remained a problem.

"Admiral," he said suddenly, "what about taking over the job of governor?"

"But, Mr. President," protested the Admiral, "I am a sailor, not a politician."

"Maybe," and the President smiled broadly, "but you've gotten along with Congress much better than I have."

Admiral Leahy made good in Puerto Rico, or at least as good as could have been expected, and went on from there to Vichy when the President decided that it was a good idea to have a man close to Pétain. There he did a great job, holding the old marshal in line on many occasions; and none of us was surprised when he came to the White House as the President's Chief of Staff. Until the end his ripe judgment and shrewd counsel were not the least of the President's reliances.

Judge Samuel Rosenman was another whose ability and judgment commanded the President's respect. The two had come together in the 1928 campaign, and after election the Governor named "Sammy the Rose" as his counselor. The association continued without a break even when F.D.R. entered the White House and after Sam's appointment to the New York State Supreme Court. Whenever there was an official document to be framed or an important address to be written, the Judge could be counted on to amble in.

Not that he, or any other man or men, ever "ghosted" the President's speeches. All were his own. As he went over his mail, never perfunctorily but always carefully, it was common for him to flip a letter or a report to Missy Le Hand or Grace Tully with instructions to "put that in speech material." In this way he built up a huge pile of information to draw on. Where occasion demanded, of course, it was supplemented by memoranda from the specialists. His preliminary draft was generally somewhat shapeless and very voluminous, sometimes as many as nine thousand words being assembled for a three-thousand-word address.

In earlier years this draft was generally turned over to Ray Moley for condensation, better sequence, and suggestion. After Ray's departure, Tommy Corcoran took over for a while, but the job eventually fell to Sammy the Rose, assisted during the war by Robert Sherwood, the playwright. Steve Early worked constantly in this field with all the passing personnel. When they had cut it to the required length and made their marginal notes, the President would go over it again and again, often as many as seven or eight times,

97

for he attached great importance to the spoken word. "Fireside chats" may have seemed informal, but he sweated over them.

Others of the inner circle, prized both as friends and consultants, were William O. Douglas, Robert H. Jackson, and Bernard M. Baruch. Bill Douglas' able and courageous handling of the Securities and Exchange Commission first brought him close to the White House, and Bob Jackson won F.D.R.'s regard by his work as Solicitor General. Even when all three were elevated to the Supreme Court, the President continued to rely on their wise counsel and rejoice in their companionship.

Contrary to general opinion, there was never a time when Mr. Baruch lost his place in the President's affection or forfeited his admiration. When there was a particularly tough assignment involving patient research and honest findings, Bernie was invariably the choice. His frequent disappearances from the Washington scene, usually interpreted by the correspondents as a loss of presidential favor, were his own doing. If there was a job to be done, well and good, but if not, he stayed away from the White House.

Companionship, as well as information and suggestion, was provided by the inner circle. The President, at the outset of our association, had promised me to cut out night work; but he got around the pledge by making small, informal dinners a fairly regular feature. At them there was much gay banter and generally a lively poker game; nevertheless, everything that had been done, or was about to be done, came under discussion. Many of these "bull sessions," as he called them, resulted in important decisions.

The President also cheated a bit on his fishing trips, for while he always took along his "gang," he also included Cabinet members, high officials, and, when the war came, many of his military advisers. As a result, they were not real vacations. I made no great objection, however, for the sun and sea were tonics, and good fellowship had the kick of wine, bringing out an almost boyish exuberance in the President that was hard on guests who could not take a ribbing. Once when we were off Panama, I remember, Secretary Ickes and Harry Hopkins were members of the party, and the two had been "feuding" bitterly only a short while before. At dinner one evening, when the ship's paper was brought in, all of us were naturally popeyed to read this startling front page piece:

The Blue Bonnet is anxious to pay its respects to the President's two civilian Aides aboard ship, Secretary Ickes and Hopkins. This paper remained neutral during the recent unpleasantness between these apostles of the New Deal. However we would be faithless to our readers if we failed to make a few pointed observations about their irrelative movements. We haven't seen much of Harold because the sea has been a little too much for him and just as he is about to heave into full view, his stomach gets in the way. He was born with the well-known silver spoon in his mouth (Hopkins is said to have remarked that it should have choked him then and there) and never worked a day in his life until Roosevelt put his name in a hat along with other contributors to the campaign and pulled his out.

The truth of the matter is that he hasn't worked much since—he has changed the names of a couple of dams—written a couple of books—corresponded with Senator Tydings—appointed Bob Moses—got some of Farley's stamps—given Steve Early headaches—Henry Morgenthau the ague—Wallace, writer's cramps, and Papa the pip.

Hopkins' fine figure and open mouth have been a real inspiration to the ship. He has a retiring, aesthetic quality about him that belies his advance publicity. One has but to see him playing "upstairs" in his rompers to realize that an angry word has never crossed his lips or an evil thought galloped thru his mighty brain. One can well understand how Hopkins gets the short end of the stick when the money is passed around in Washington. His case rests on justice and truth—not upon intrigue.

As we have watched this famous pair we are sure they will both go far and we are quite confident of the place—the ash can!

Only when the President burst out laughing did we tumble to the fact that it was a "rib." Harry took it as a great joke, and the Old Curmudgeon, after a few painful gulps, actually cracked a smile. These outings, of course, came to an end on the outbreak of war, and soon became a memory along with laughter and relaxation.

CHAPTER VIII

THE LOAD GROWS HEAVIER

FROM MY POINT OF VIEW, AT LEAST, THE FIRST FOUR years passed off in satisfactory fashion; for, while the President worked harder than I liked, he showed no signs of strain and kept to his schedule except in minor details. The New Deal seemed to be off to a flying start, for he had the support of public sentiment and the co-operation of Congress. Upsets were discounted by the enthusiasm of planning and the optimism of his sanguine temperament.

Although he was a bit too heavy, weighing around 190, every check showed him organically sound. His feet, in bad shape at the time he came under my care, had been built up by massage and his own patient exercises, and there was also considerable improvement in his legs. In the pool, with water below his armpits, he could go it alone, and there was a proud day, early in 1937, when he walked a hundred yards without other aid than a supporting arm. One of his braces might have been discarded had he been a private citizen, but I dared not take the risk of a fall and possible fracture with the President of the United States.

The 1936 campaign was what the race-track gentry call a "breeze," proving more of a vacation than a task. It was not that the President held Governor Landon in less than respect and esteem as a man of character and ability, for in the years that followed he gave many evidences of his friendship and admiration. It was simply that he thought it stupid of the Republicans to pick a nominee with so little background, so far removed from the national scene, who would have to be identified to an audience every time he made a speech. At no time during the campaign did he have the least doubt of the result, although the size of his electoral vote was surprising.

With the campaign out of the way, the President at the peak of his popularity and in fine shape both physically and mentally, I put by all of my old anxieties and looked forward to four nice, easy, pleasant years. Where the first bad break came was in the spring months of 1937 when he initiated the so-called "court-packing" bill. As a nonpolitical Navy man, it is not for me to go into the merits of the proposal, but there are certain observations that I think it my right to make. Instead of hugging it as a secret until the last second and then firing it as a bombshell, he made his ideas the subject of fairly wide discussion. In the issue of *Collier's* under date of December 26, 1936, for example, he O.K.'d an authoritative statement that gave his intent in full detail. Because of the explicitness with which the plan was outlined, as well as the light it throws on the President's thought, I think the following quotation well worth while:

Always frank, he [the President] has been particularly frank in the statement of his belief that there is no place in the United States for the twilight zone that now stretches between the Government and the States, a dreary, tragic No Man's Land exempted by judicial interpretation from control either by federal law or state statute. Today, as in the past, he insists that there are needed standards in many social and economic areas that *must* be national. ... From every part of the country is coming a demand for a constitutional amendment that will give the federal government the right to exercise control over this twilight zone, this No Man's Land. Not an encroachment on states' rights, but the assertion of federal authority over vast domains into which the states do not and cannot reach. ... But is a constitutional amendment necessary, after all, for the attainment of New Deal objectives?

Every true American reveres the Constitution, but, regrettably, very few have ever read it. The President accompanies his reverence by full knowledge, for he can come close to repeating the great document. What impresses him as it must impress every other student, is the very evident effort of the fathers of the republic to deal with the needs of their times as those needs arose. ... Failures having made them conscious of the fact that old needs passed and new needs rose, the framers were explicit when and wherever possible, and broadly general in other cases.

Take the Preamble, for instance. People regard it as a mere rhetorical flourish, and yet it is as integral a part of the Constitution as any article. "We, the People of the United States, in Order to form a more perfect Union, establish Justice, insure domestic tranquillity, provide for the common defense, *promote the general welfare,* and secure the blessings of Liberty to ourselves and our Posterity, do ordain and establish this Constitution for the United States of America." What is that if not a plain statement of purpose?

Article I, Section 1, provides that "all legislative Powers herein granted shall be vested in a Congress of the United States," and Section 8, after setting forth that "the Congress shall have Power to lay and collect taxes, Duties, Imposts and Excises, and provide for the common defense and *General Welfare* of the United States," goes on to list other powers. In fact, the framers would seem to have racked their brains to set down every national need, and then, out of their consciousness that other needs were bound to rise, added this paragraph; "To make all Laws which shall be necessary and proper for carrying into Execution the foregoing Powers, and *all other Powers* vested by this Constitution in the Government of the United States, or in department or officer thereof." What plainer than that "all other powers" carries with it explicit authorization to enact laws to "promote the General Welfare" so specifically mentioned in the Preamble and again in Article I, Section 1?

Article III, Section 1, states simply that "the judicial Power of the United States shall be vested in one Supreme Court, and in such inferior Courts as the Congress may from time to time ordain and establish." Not one word that gives the Supreme Court any power to override the legislative branch.

Is Congress, therefore, as powerless as has been assumed? Many important decisions yet remain to be handed down by the Supreme Court, notably with reference to the Social Security Act and the Wagner Labor Act. What, for instance, if these and other New Deal laws are held unconstitutional, thereby affirming the right of the judicial branch to override the legislative branch, could Congress do?

There is one thing that it could do without question, and that is the passage of a statute taking away from all inferior federal courts the right to pass on questions of constitutionality, and directing them to certify all such cases to the Supreme Court of the United States, where it would be mandatory to put them on a preferred docket for the earliest possible decision.

There is still another arrow in the Congressional quiver. If the coming session witnesses the adoption of a housing bill, or a bill providing for maximum hours and minimum wages, or a bill relating to sweatshops and child labor, or the new Guffey coal bill, each of these acts could have a rider attached *charging* the Supreme Court to bear in mind that the law was enacted pursuant to the Constitutional provision vesting all legislative power in the Congress, and explicitly authorizing it "to provide for the general welfare of the United States."

If this proves ineffective, Congress can *enlarge* the Supreme Court, increasing the number of justices from nine to twelve or fifteen. The power is beyond cavil, for three changes have been made in the number of justices. We started out with six and have had as many as ten.

105

The President not only authorized this statement of his views but read the article after its preparation and pointed out the words he wanted italicized. Three months after its publication, and when extended conferences had shown the hopelessness of any other remedy, he asked Congress for the enlargement of the Supreme Court to end what, in his opinion, was a blind alley as far as laws to "provide for the general welfare" were concerned.

A bold step, in the opinion of a good many of his advisers, but he justified it by pointing to this paragraph in the Constitution: "He [the President] shall from time to time give to the Congress information of the State of the Union, and recommend to their consideration such measures as he shall judge necessary and expedient." As he saw it, the Congress was made up of men primarily concerned with their own constituencies, their own local popularity, and it was only the President, representing the whole people, who could speak for the nation, suggesting and urging laws that he deemed to be in the national interest.

It was a bitter fight, and he gave to it everything he had, pushing his routine to one side and devoting his nights as well as days to conference, argument, and strategy. Tommy Corcoran's reports on his poll of the Senate were overly optimistic, and the President was not prepared for the defeat of his proposal. The final vote came as a hard blow and did not help him to repair the bad effects of the battle.

A second bad break came in 1938 when the President attempted to purge certain Democratic senators who had stoutly opposed several New Deal measures. Politically wise Jim Farley, as chairman of the National Committee, advised against it, but F.D.R. could not be dissuaded. Regarding himself as the authoritative head of the party and with a mandate from the people, he viewed opposition by Democrats to major administration measures much as the captain of a ship would view mutiny on the high seas. Not only did he think that party discipline was involved but also the party's good faith. Moreover, the measures fought by these senators happened to be closest to his heart.

The purge trips, I am sure, will always be remembered as nightmares by those who accompanied the President. Particularly the speech in a small Georgia town before the constituents of Walter George. With Senator George sitting on the platform, so close that he could have been touched, the President recited the Georgian's antagonism to various New Deal bills and calmly asked for his defeat. It was a warm day, but you could feel the ice forming as the people sat in angry silence. The invasion of Maryland, where the President also spoke against Senator Millard Tydings, was no less embarrassing and futile. All that the purge did was to provoke bitternesses that never died out.

After this defeat I hoped for a slowing-down that would build him up again, but foreign affairs began to put unceasing pressure on his time and strength.

Although too much of a realist to believe in the efficacy of the League of Nations as it had turned out, the President still held firmly to his faith in some form of international concert as the one sure road to world peace. This faith was the inspiration for the Good Neighbor policy that now began to occupy his mind. With the New World united and the twenty-one republics of the Western Hemisphere standing shoulder to shoulder in fraternal union, what proof more convincing to the peoples of earth that international accord was not an impossibility was needed?

A strong navy was commanded by common sense, but even as the President urged the construction of an adequate fleet, so did he seek to make clear America's pacific intentions and passion for peace. Drastic neutrality legislation that outlawed war profits was followed by the voluntary surrender of long-asserted neutral rights that were an invitation to war. Our agreement with France and Great Britain paved the way for international monetary stabilization, and the approval of his reciprocal tariff policy permitted the President to push forward the work of the Trade Agreements Section, not only to recapture our foreign commerce but to strike a leveling blow at the artificial barriers that made for international irritation.

There are still those who believe that the President was fooled by the Japanese, swallowing their lies about peaceful intent right up to Pearl Harbor. On the contrary, he became convinced that Japan's militarists were on the march as early as 1936, when their armies began the manufacture of "incidents" in China.

Back in 1919 I was a medical officer on the U.S.S. *New Orleans,* playing a small part in the ill-fated attempt of the Allies to support Admiral Kolchak's counterrevolutionary drive against the Bolsheviks. When I happened to mention it to the President, he pumped me dry about Manchuria and Eastern Siberia and the attitude of the Japanese at that time. When I told him of their arrogance and brutal aggressions, he nodded his head. "Yes," he said, "the Japanese are the Prussians of the East, and just as drunk with their dream of dominion. They mean to have Manchuria, nor will it stop there. After China will come the conquest of the British and Dutch possessions in the Pacific, and eventually a smash at the Philippines."

Look over the record, and you will find that he left no stone unturned to strengthen our defenses in the Pacific and in the Canal Zone. Nor will it do to forget his famous "quarantine" speech made at the dedication of a bridge in Chicago on October 6, 1937. It was expected that he would deal only with conservation and the control of waterways, but when he began the preparation of his address, he confided to a few of us that he meant to take cognizance of the Japanese menace to world peace. The decision was kept a profound secret, and I can still see the open mouths of the audience as the President let loose with these statements:

109

"The peace, the freedom, and the security of 90 per cent of the population of the world is being jeopardized by the remaining 10 per cent who are threatening a breakdown of all international law and order. Today the 90 per cent want to live in peace under law and in accordance with moral standards that have received almost universal acceptance through the centuries, and can and must find some way to make their will prevail. It seems to be unfortunately true that the epidemic of world lawlessness is spreading. When an epidemic of physical disease starts to spread, the community approves and joins in a quarantine of the patients in order to protect the health of the community against the spread of the disease."

As an opening gun in the campaign for preparedness, the speech was a dud, the only result being a bitter attack on the President as a warmonger who wanted to "send American boys to fight and die in foreign lands." Even the sinking of the *Panay* worked no great change in public sentiment, and Congress turned a deaf ear to his plea for a larger and more effective air force. As late as 1939 we had just seven aircraft carriers.

Undiscouraged, he drove hard at both the Army and the Navy, demanding the experimentation and research that would lead to improvement. Night after night I watched him working away on rough designs for giving ships greater defensive strength, and just as he first suggested cruisers of the *Guam* and *Alaska* class, so was the *Independence* type of airplane carrier his brain child. He also kept after the Army. And hardly a day passed that General Watson did not go over to the War Department with F.D.R.'s ideas for some improvement in munitions.

At no time did the President fool himself as to the character of Adolf Hitler. He had read *Mein Kampf*, talking it over with us many an evening, and was never in doubt as to the force and deadly purpose of the Fuehrer. As a student of history and one who had traveled in Germany, he knew the sheeplike quality of the German people and their passion for medicine men, incantations, and tom-toms. He viewed Munich as a surrender that would only whet Hitler's appetite for conquest. "Appeasement," he declared, "is on the same level as fear, and a fear policy invites war as surely as a provocative policy." He prophesied the march into Czechoslovakia, and when the Germans occupied Memel one week later, he made the flat prediction that the invasion of Poland was only a question of time.

Although hopeful that the United States might escape involvement in the second World War that he foresaw so plainly, the President felt that preparedness was commanded by every sound instinct of self-preservation. He lost his fight for the fortification of Guam but succeeded in gaining approval for new naval and air bases at Midway, Wake, Johnston, and Palmyra Islands, and in the Aleutians. Congress also began to turn a more willing ear to his pleas for a larger and more modern navy.

Any doubt that the President may have had as to Hitler's true intent was removed on the evening of August 25, 1939. I had persuaded him to leave the White House for a rest, and we were in Newfoundland waters at the time. After a day in pursuit of salmon we were sitting around the dinner table, swapping tall tales about the big ones that had got away, when suddenly a message alerted all hands and kept us up for the rest of the night. Its source was the Turkish News Service, but London did the transmitting.

Flatly, unqualifiedly, the message stated that Hitler had decided on the immediate invasion of Poland. A bargain with Russia, already signed and sealed, would free Germany from any fear of the Red armies, and not more than three weeks would be required for the conquest of Poland. England and France, of course, would spring to the aid of the Poles, both by reason of treaty obligations and their own safety, but Germany counted on their unreadiness.

A lightning stroke would crush Belgium and Holland, and after that a smash into France and a pounce on Denmark and Norway. Then a holding operation, designed to keep Great Britain at bay while German armies invaded the Balkans with Italy coming into the war as a full Axis partner. From the Balkans on to Palestine, a return to the Kaiser's "Berlin to Bagdad" dream, followed by a drive across the Mediterranean into North Africa, a juncture with the Italians in Tripoli and Tunis, and finally an irresistible sweep into Egypt. These objectives attained, an attack in force on beleaguered England. Fantastic at the time, and yet marching events soon proved that the Turkish News Service was accurate in all but one detail—Hitler's break with Russia.

The President gave orders at once for a return to Washington, but heavy fog cut down our speed, and it was not until August 30 that we reached the White House. On September 1 the German armies raced into Poland, and seventeen days later, as the Poles stood with their backs to the Pripet marshes, Russia invaded from the East.

CHAPTER IX

WHY A THIRD TERM

WITH THE INVASION OF POLAND THERE BEGAN A battle with the President that continued to the day of his death. As clearly as though gifted with clairvoyance, he saw the menace of Hitler's megalomania, backed by the might of German armies and the military genius of the German General Staff. More and more he drove himself relentlessly, and every day was a fight to make him stick to his schedule.

On the outbreak of hostilities, as required by the Neutrality Act, the President embargoed shipments of arms to any of the belligerent nations but immediately called a special session of Congress to repeal the embargo provision. Here again was another exhausting battle, for a powerful segment of public opinion still clung to the belief that the Atlantic and Pacific were barriers. The President directed the fight from start to finish, and on November 4 the act was amended to permit England and France to buy our arms for cash and carry them away in their own ships.

There was a night during the debate, after a small

and informal dinner at the White House, when the President talked frankly about his own feelings with respect to England and the English. A great people, in his opinion, brought up in a great tradition and holding to it with a tenacity that defied party politics. To every Briton the Empire was a religion, and any threat to it welded them into phalanx formation.

On the other hand, often an irritating people, by reason of a conviction of superiority so ingrained and perfected by time as to transcend mere egotism. Likewise a shrewd, hard-bargaining people, aggressive territorially and in every trade relation, and in time of peace it was highly necessary to be on constant guard to keep them from taking our eyeteeth. Nevertheless, a steadfast people, a people kin to us by blood, holding to the same ideals, and an assured ally of the United States in event of international discord. A conquered England, her land and shores in the possession of Germany, meant the end of America's security, therefore England *had* to be saved.

Later on, when the Lend-Lease was being debated, the President stated his position in this simple, homely phrase: "Suppose my neighbor's house catches fire and I have a length of garden hose four or five hundred feet away. If I can take my garden hose and connect it up with his hydrant, I may help him to put out the fire and thus save my own house."

Remedying our own pitiful unpreparedness became a major activity. Declaring a state of emergency, the

President called in the heads of the armed services and studied the best methods of building up reserves. One of his direct orders, I recall, started the production of antiaircraft guns on a large scale. Even the cry of "warmonger" did not swerve him from his purpose to strengthen the national defense.

From the first shot the President had feared Italy's entrance on the side of Germany, and for a time he had high hopes that Mussolini could be persuaded to maintain neutrality. The word that he had failed came on the morning of the day that he was to address the graduating class of the University of Virginia. Immediately, and over the protest of State Department officials, he reached for his prepared speech and added this fiery sentence: "On this tenth day of June, 1940, the hand that held the dagger has struck it into the back of its neighbor."

The President had been suffering for some days from clogged sinuses, and on his return that night, came at once to my office in the White House basement. While I was giving him treatment, Harry Hopkins and Adolf Berle arrived, the latter bringing the draft of a new neutrality proclamation. Both commented on the "dagger in the back" phrase; and F.D.R., eyes fairly blazing, said that few things had ever given him more intense satisfaction than the open expression of his anger at an "evil and unjustified action."

From the first the President had viewed the French

situation with alarm, for while ardent in his admiration for the people, he was without confidence in their leaders. All of them, in his opinion, were thinking in terms of political advantage—"quarreling about power like dogs over a bone"—and no strong man of the Clemenceau type was emerging. Even so, France's sudden collapse astounded him, for he had believed that the army could and would fight.

Marshal Pétain's request for an armistice strengthened his conviction that the democracies of the world were in deadly danger from the hosts of totalitarianism, and that it was more and more vital for the United States to make common cause with those who were struggling against the "gods of force and hate." When, therefore, Mr. Churchill begged for help, the call fell on receptive ears, nor did the President need to be told of Britain's desperate plight. All of her tanks, trucks, and artillery had been left on the beaches at Dunkirk, and thousands of her best fighting men. Half of the destroyer fleet had been put out of action, and German planes and U-boats were sinking many merchant ships. Still more menacing, there was the word that 2,500 German barges were gathering for a Channel crossing.

What came into the President's mind at once was the two-hundred-odd First-World-War destroyers lying idle and useless in American ports. A swift survey of his powers discovered that he had the right to transfer, exchange, or sell any and all naval material "not essential to the defense of the United States." A second step was to devise some plan by which a certain number of these destroyers could be handed over to the British without exciting too much opposition in Congress and stirring America Firsters to new outbreaks.

Many of our fishing trips had carried us into Newfoundland waters, the Bahamas, and the Caribbean, and in 1936 we paid a very thorough visit of inspection to Trinidad. At the time he had spread a map on the table and pointed out the bases—Newfoundland, Bermuda, Jamaica, Santa Lucia, Antigua, and Trinidad—that were necessary to guard the Western Hemisphere against attack. Now, as a means of coming to Britain's aid, he suggested the transfer of fifty old destroyers in exchange for ninety-nine-year leases on the required bases.

Even with the press of other preoccupations he followed each of those destroyers to the war's end. In March 1942, it may be remembered, the aged *Buchanan* steamed into Saint-Nazaire, then Germany's principal submarine and battleship base, and after letting go with all her guns, rammed at full speed into the main lock gate, putting it out of commission. The President's pride in the exploit was unbounded, and at later meetings with Mr. Churchill he loved to count up the U-boats that our "old wrecks" had sent to the bottom.

After the collapse of France, and with the German

drive gathering even more irresistible speed, the President made no pretense of keeping to his schedule with respect to diet, rest periods, and daily exercise. As always when under pressure, he ate luncheon at his desk, cut out his swims, and worked late into the night. The best that I could do was to guard against deterioration. Aside from loss of weight, however, and deeper lines in his face, physical examinations developed no danger signs.

What distressed him was the persistence of the myth that Europe was none of our business. Seeing the peril so clearly himself, he took blame for his failure to give equal vision to the people as a whole. Many eminent Republicans saw eye to eye with him in his belief that the war in Europe *was* our business, but more and more he became convinced that the party itself still held to isolationism, and that a Republican victory meant a return to "hermit" policies. It was this conviction, and nothing else, that impelled him to put aside his personal desires and stand for a third term.

I am not guessing or "hindsighting" when I say this: Until he realized the full extent of Hitler's paranoia, the President discussed his plans for retirement with me in many confidential talks. I recall with particular vividness this specific statement, made not just once but often: "On January 21, 1941, when a new man takes over, I'll be in Hyde Park having the time of my life." He had loved his years in the White House, but after two strenuous terms he looked forward with eagerness to the quiet of country life with leisure for the writing he had in mind.

It was not only the whys and hows of the New Deal that he wanted to set down as an authoritative contribution to history, but it was also his purpose to comment on the current political scene. W. L. Chenery, editor of *Collier's*, had been urging him to become a regular contributor after retirement, and I happen to know that negotiations were well along when the President broke them off by reason of his decision to stand for a third term.

More than anything else, however, my stays at Hyde Park convinced me that he was absolutely sincere in his desire to quit public office. Love for the place went down to the roots of his being. The planting had been done under his personal supervision, and every tree was dear to him. He had laid out the roads and could drive his car around winding turns and through the thickly wooded sections without brushing the fender. The Secret Service men always followed him, of course, and it delighted him to lose them in some tangle of byways.

The selected cutting of his hardwood trees paid the taxes on nonarable areas, and where the acreage was no good for crops, he had planted spruce cedars that brought a nice return when sold as Christmas trees. He knew husbandry and forestry and had even made bee culture a study, talking enthusiastically about the development of strains and grades of honey. Once he worked up quite an excitement over D.D.T., the new insecticide, but it subsided quickly when I told him that it would kill his bees as well as Japanese beetles.

More and more, as his second term neared the end, he talked of Hyde Park, telling of the things he meant to do "when I've put Washington behind me." Where was there any motive for deceiving me? I was not a politician to be hoodwinked, and not a gossip that might be expected to run out and spread the news. Even if it be conceded that my nonpolitical Navy life had made me trustful and naïve, certainly no such charge can be leveled against Charles Michelson. Hard-bitten and realistic after years in the newspaper game, he was also an "insider" by reason of his long tenure as director of publicity for the Democratic National Committee.

Writing in 1939 for a national magazine, this veteran observer and skilled analyst gave the following judgment on what might happen in 1940:

My guess is that Franklin D. Roosevelt would take a case of the hives rather than four years more of the headache that being President means. It will not be as easy a choice as that. Circumstances might arise that would make it impossible for him to lay down the burden. The world might be at war with or without threat of our involvement, or some other equally acute emergency might eventuate that would forbid a change of administration, and the man in the White House is not the kind

121

of individual who would let his personal desires interfere with what seemed to him to be his duty.

That is exactly what happened. At first party leaders, fearful of the third-term tradition, respected the President's purpose to retire, but it was not long before they switched to frantic insistence on renomination. The world situation, of course, had something to do with it, but I think that the real reason was the lack of any other strong candidate. Cordell Hull was given consideration for a while, but aside from his own disinclination to leave the State Department, there was the feeling that his health would not permit him to make a sufficiently vigorous campaign.

Partisan considerations, however, had no weight with the President, and just as he continued to tell me that he would not be a candidate, so did he give others the same assurance. I have no doubt that Jim Farley is perfectly correct in his statement that Mr. Roosevelt, in a private talk at Hyde Park well in advance of the convention, said explicitly that he had no intention of seeking a third term.

What changed his mind was the circumstances so shrewdly pointed out by Charlie Michelson. Every sign indicated a repudiation of his foreign policy in event of Republican victory, and that victory looked to be certain unless he himself took the field and made the fight in person. While absolutely sincere in his belief that the United States *could* keep out of the war, he believed that the one and only means to achieve that end was to strengthen the Allies by every means in American power. But would a Republican administration see it that way?

There was also the consideration that it was no time to take a chance on untried leadership. For eight years his hand had been at the helm, and behind him was the accumulated experience of those years, both with respect to international problems as well as domestic.

Was it his right to quit in accordance with his desires, or was it his *obligation* to let the people balance his offer of continued conduct against the claim of another? Finally deciding that the decision was not individual but one to be made by the men and women of America, he consented to make the race. If the people wanted him, he would serve; if not, he could lay down the load without self-reproach.

The question of a running mate now rose to irk him. The President had a very real affection for Jack Garner and held him in high esteem for his character and abilities, but the Texan had no liking for many New Deal measures in the beginning and liked them less as the years went by. Another candidate, better disposed to the President's declared policies, had to be chosen, and quite a boom developed for William Bankhead of Alabama, then Speaker of the House. It happened, however, that I knew Congressman Bankhead to be suffering from a fatal ailment, but this

123

could not be told, and the President's failure to select him caused considerable bitterness.

How the name of Henry Wallace came up I cannot remember. He had never been close to the President, in the sense of being invited to the small dinners and poker parties; nor was he ever taken on fishing trips, prize proof of intimacy. Nevertheless the President liked Secretary Wallace for his wholehearted support of every New Deal bill, and several times made mention of his "capacity for growth." What moved him mainly, I think, was his belief that Wallace's nomination would please the farmers and give the ticket strength in agricultural areas.

A good deal of confusion marked the preconvention period. Having consented to make the race if drafted, and after agreeing on Henry Wallace, the President seemingly dismissed the matter from his thought and gave entire attention to international affairs. With Jim Farley, chairman of the Democratic National Committee, open in his opposition to a third term, Harry Hopkins bustled out to Chicago to handle things. Unthinkingly, rather than deliberately, he ignored Mr. Farley for several days, a blunder that stirred the bitter resentment of Jim's many friends. This and the insistence on Wallace's nomination aroused a lot of feeling, and the cry of "phony draft" began to be raised.

The President's reaction was instant and angry. Overwork had left him tired and edgy, and his usual evenness of disposition had been replaced by a very definite irritability. The climax came in the very hour of his nomination. Steve Early and I had slipped away from the White House for a bite of dinner at a downtown restaurant, but before we had a chance to taste the soup, Pa Watson telephoned an urgent message to return at once.

We found him waiting for us, pacing up and down the corridor, and were told in one of his loud whispers that "hell was poppin'." The Boss, Pa went on to explain, had his Dutch up, and was going to refuse to run. It was not only the "phony draft" attack, but the bedlam of disapproval that broke out when Henry Wallace's name was put in nomination. But for rapid action by the chairman, Paul McNutt would have been named, a direct blow at the President. Entering the study, we found F.D.R., set of jaw, writing away on a desk pad. Missy Le Hand, Grace Tully, and Sam Rosenman huddled in a corner, gaped helplessly. He waved us off impatiently when we tried to talk, and after throwing down his pencil, handed the sheet to Judge Rosenman.

"Put that in shape, Sam," he ordered, "and give it out. No," he continued, turning to us, "I've made up my mind. I did not want to run, and now some of the very people who urged me the most are putting me in the position of an office-hungry politician, scheming and plotting to keep his job. I'm through. Go on, Sam, and do as I've told you."

General Watson, Steve, and I followed the Judge out of the room, and in the corridor Pa reached out a hamlike paw and snatched the sheet of paper away from Sam. That gave all of us spirit enough to march back in and lay down a barrage of argument. Hadn't the nomination been made on the first ballot? And didn't it prove that the overwhelming majority of the delegates were for him? Surely he knew enough about politics to know that Democrats were never unanimous on anything. And Henry Wallace, after all, was a rather large pill for the conservatives to swallow, considering that he was not well known to the party's rank and file. We hammered away at him for the best part of an hour, and in the end he smiled somewhat sheepishly and admitted that he had gone off half-cocked. Thank the Lord, he did not ask what had become of the refusal he had written out.

Nevertheless, the President showed no large enthusiasm for the race, turning down Ed Flynn's plea for speeches. As the campaign warmed up, however, with Wendell Willkie beginning to exhibit the force that had marked his earlier addresses, F.D.R.'s eyes lighted with the old battle fire, and party leaders had no quarrel with him from that time on. Back in 1936 he had not taken Governor Landon very seriously, but Mr. Willkie was something else again. His meteoric climb proved that he had caught the popular imagination, and there was no question as to his ability. F.D.R., in fact, liked him and admired him, and lamented his untimely death as a distinct loss to America's public life.

Before a month had passed, however, the President had lost all doubt as to the result. The Old Guard sulked in their tents, damning Mr. Willkie as "another Roosevelt," and every report showed that the Republicans lacked an effective organization. Huge meetings and tumultuous enthusiasm, while impressive, were no substitute for the machinery necessary to get out the vote. When the election returns told F.D.R. that he had been returned for a third term, he was deeply moved by the proof of popular confidence but not elated. Better than anyone he knew what lay ahead.

Sitting down with the President soon after the inauguration, the two of us made his physical condition the subject of detailed discussion. Head to foot checkups were more than satisfactory; but, as I pointed out, another four years of wearing effort precluded all hope of improvement. The very best that could be expected was the prevention of deterioration, and this called for a return to his routine and strict adherence to rules of daily conduct. After listening carefully to what he must do and what he could not do, the President nodded his head, and we shook hands on the agreement.

Even so, there was the job that had to be done, and the increase in pressure was steady and relentless. After a crowded day it became more and more his habit to go over stacked papers in the evening, penciling comment, suggestions, instructions, and decisions. It did not seem possible that human strength could stand the strain, but always he seemed to find new wells of the spirit on which to draw.

By the end of 1940 the British were scraping the bottom of the Treasury barrel, and Hitler was jubilantly announcing that spring would see the end of the war. Lending them millions was not the answer, and during the course of extended discussions, the President advanced the brand-new theory that it might be possible for us to *build* and *manufacture,* and then *lease.* As always, he tried it out on the country in a fireside chat; and when it had a favorable reception, he came forward with the direct proposal of the Lend-Lease measure that will stand for all time as the one thing that saved the Old World from Hitler's rule, and possibly prevented a like fate from befalling the Western Hemisphere.

CHAPTER X

THE ATLANTIC CHARTER

ABOVE AND BEYOND THE WEIGHT OF DOMESTIC PROB-lems that lay on the President, there was the terrifying march of Hitler's armed hordes across the map of Europe, and his fear that Germany's paranoiac dream of world dominion might yet involve the United States. From the first shot of war in Europe, his mind concerned itself with the need for some statement of faith—an affirmation of democratic belief—that would serve to hearten and strengthen the peoples of earth in their fight against totalitarianism. All of us close to him knew that this was in the back of his thought, pushing to the front whenever the burdens of the day permitted.

In the message to Congress on January 6, 1941, he had set forth his Four Freedoms—freedom of speech and worship, and freedom from want and from aggression—but he made frank admission of their generality. Something more specific was needed, not necessarily in such detail as Woodrow Wilson's Fourteen Points but still a ringing declaration that would make clear the position and principles of the United States.

Throughout the spring he was more reserved than usual, less inclined for company, and it worried me no little. When we left Washington on August 3, however, supposedly for a fishing trip, I noted a recovery of his usual gaiety of spirit and put it down to the lift that a vacation at sea always gave him. Not until the historic meeting with England's Prime Minister and the proclamation of the Atlantic Charter did I realize that the change was due to the fact that he had decided on a course of action.

There was nothing about the start of the trip to make us think that it was other than the usual thing. Just Pa Watson, Captain Jack Beardall, his naval aide, and myself, all tried and true fishermen, made up the party. Going by train to New London, the President took a look at the submarine base and then boarded the *Potomac* for Buzzard's Bay. On the morning of the fourth we picked up Crown Princess Martha of Norway, Prince Karl of Sweden, and four or five other royal exiles, and after a day of angling the President took them ashore, handling the wheel of a speedboat himself.

That night we steamed away to Martha's Vineyard, and early on the morning of the fifth transferred to the U.S.S. *Augusta*. We learned afterward that the *Potomac* kept on up to Cape Cod and New England waters, still flying the President's flag and giving no indication that he was not on board. The switch occa-

sioned curiosity, of course, especially when we found
General Marshall, Admiral King, and Admiral Stark
on board the *Augusta,* but it was not satisfied until
we anchored off the Argentia Base in Newfoundland
on the morning of the seventh. Then, and only then,
did the President tell us of the coming conference with
Prime Minister Churchill.

Soon after anchoring, more members of the American team came pouring in. Major General Henry Arn-
old, Major General James Burns, and Rear Admiral
Richmond Turner came over to the *Augusta* from the
Tuscaloosa, and Undersecretary of State Sumner
Welles and Averill Harriman arrived by plane. These
were followed by Ensign Franklin Roosevelt, Jr., and
Captain Elliott Roosevelt, assigned to additional duty
as presidential aides that their father might have a
visit with his sons.

H.M.S. *Prince of Wales* stood in on the morning of
the ninth, and dropped anchor close to the *Augusta.*
Soon afterward the Prime Minister came aboard,
bearing a letter to the President from King George
and accompanied by his staff and Harry Hopkins.
Harry, reaching London after a week in Moscow with
Marshal Stalin, had been given a ride to the rendezvous by Mr. Churchill.

One look at the Prime Minister's company made us
know that he had come prepared for full discussion of
every possible topic. As political advisers, he had Sir
Alexander Cadogan, Permanent Undersecretary of

State for Foreign Affairs, Lord Cherwell, and several others. A large Admiralty party was headed by Admiral of the Fleet Sir Dudley Pound, the War Office party by General Sir John Dill, the Air Ministry party by Air Chief Marshal Sir Wilfrid Freeman, and there were also representatives from the Office of the Ministry of Defense. Altogether a most imposing array.

It was our first sight of the Prime Minister, and all of us, from the President down, felt the force and charm of the man. In the many meetings with him that followed—Washington, Quebec, Casablanca, Cairo, Teheran, Malta, and Yalta—I never lost the sense of profound admiration, but the time did arrive when, as White House physician, I looked on "Winnie" as Public Enemy Number One. It was his invariable habit to take a nap after luncheon, and nothing was allowed to interfere with it. At the various conferences, if too far away from his own room, he would borrow some other for his daily snooze. As a consequence, he was ready and willing to sit up all night, puffing away on his big cigar and flanked by a glass of Scotch. He was a tremendously stimulating companion whom the President liked and enjoyed, and although I always asked that eleven o'clock be set as a dead line, it was rarely observed.

The President and the Prime Minister lunched together, and the long discussion was followed by another that evening after a formal dinner on the *Augusta* for all of the "brass," both British and American. The real start of the conference, however, was divine service on the quarter-deck of the *Prince of Wales* the following day. The President and the Prime Minister attended with their staffs, and some 250 bluejackets and Marines from our ships stood side by side with the British ship's company. The pulpit was decked with the colors of both countries, and an American chaplain joined with a British chaplain in conducting prayers. I have never listened to a more inspiring religious service, and I know that every heart swelled as a thousand voices sang "Our God, Our Help in Ages Past," "Onward, Christian Soldiers," and "Eternal Father, Strong to Save." As we went back to the *Augusta*, the President said that what we had just heard would, in his opinion, be the keynote of the conference.

The sessions that began at once continued almost without a break through Tuesday. While the President and Mr. Churchill had not met before, telephone conversation and correspondence had given them a taste of each other's quality, and the meeting of minds was instant. Even so, a good deal of fencing was inevitable, for the Prime Minister wanted far more than the President was willing to give.

Mr. Churchill, quite understandably, desired some declaration that would indicate a hard and fast Anglo-American alliance. Mr. Roosevelt, with the United States still at peace, had no mind to go further than a statement of common purposes and principles in the peace that would follow war. During the three days of continuous discussion, he held unchangeably to his position, and the Atlantic Charter, as finally framed, expressed his thought without a single major deviation.

The two first drafts of the document—the British and the American—were turned over to Sumner Welles and Sir Alexander Cadogan, and after being boiled down to one, the single version came up for final discussion. The President, talking that night, reported that Mr. Churchill had been most generous in his concessions to the American position, but laughed a bit at the Prime Minister's liking for sonorous phrases. "At that," he admitted, "some of his changes had more force than my own more homely way of putting it."

Russia, as a matter of course, figured largely in the discussions, for the conference covered military matters as well as the Charter. With his usual vision, the President had prophesied from the very start that the Russo-German alliance would not last. Hitler, he contended, could not possibly permit Stalin and his Communists to lord it over the Baltic and the Balkans, and would turn on his ally at the first propitious moment. Under his instructions Sumner Welles had been conducting conversations with Constantin Oumansky, the Russian Ambassador in Washington, trying to drive a wedge between the two mismated partners and at the same time laying a foundation for working relations with Marshal Stalin when the break did come.

When Germany invaded Russia, therefore, Moscow was not only agreeable to Harry Hopkins' visit but entirely willing to open up Russian resources for his inspection. It was what he had seen and heard that Harry reported, first to the President and then to the Prime Minister and the assembled staffs. Stalin, he said, had pledged resistance to the last man. It was highly probable that the Russians would be driven deep into the interior, but Moscow would never be taken nor Russian resistance broken. And given the aid of American guns, munitions, and mechanized equipment, a tremendous counteroffensive could be expected.

The President and the Prime Minister were convinced, and even the hard-boiled generals and admirals admitted that the Hopkins report had materially changed their views as to Russia's ability to withstand the sweep of Hitler's panzer divisions. As a result, Mr. Churchill and F.D.R. addressed a joint letter to Marshal Stalin that pledged early and continuing assistance, both military and economic. On that cheerful note the conference adjourned.

An incident of the meeting is worth recalling as evidence of the alertness and retentiveness of the President's mind. One evening Lord Cherwell talked at some length about the development of new forms of energy. What intrigued the President particularly was the rumor that a type of bomb, blasting laterally as well as downward with equal force and able to scatter destruction over a circumference of two miles, was being developed by the enemy! From that day on, the mystery bomb was added to the President's long list of interests; and when, at a later date, the decision as to atomic fission was put up to him, he gave the order to gamble two billions without hesitancy.

The meeting with Mr. Churchill and the world's favorable reception of the Charter sent F.D.R. back to Washington in top form. But soon the rising menace of Japan began to claim his attention, and then came the fateful morning of December 7.

To all of us who were closest to the President at the time of Pearl Harbor—the intimate White House circle—nothing is more outrageous than the attempt to prove that he expected the Japanese attack, and in fact, had even invited it as the one sure way to plunge the country into the war that he wanted. Not even Washington or Lincoln was ever accused more infamously, for the charge stained his hands with American blood and made him the murderer of every boy who fell in battle on sea or land.

We knew that he was deeply concerned over the unsatisfactory nature of Nomura's and Kurusu's conversations with Secretary Hull; yet it was his firm conviction that even the madness of Japan's military masters would not risk a war with the United States. It might well be that they would take advantage of Great Britain's extremity and strike at Singapore or some other point in the Far East, but an attack on any

American possession did not enter his thought. I sat with him on that Sunday morning from ten to twelve o'clock, while Mr. Hull was waiting over in the State Department for the Japanese envoys to bring their government's reply to the American note, and the President made it clear that he counted only on the usual evasions.

Going home, I was at luncheon when the White House telephone operator gave me the news of Pearl Harbor and the President's request to report at once. Pa Watson was in Charlottesville, and Admiral Leahy could not be found; so Steve Early and I took over. Captain Beardall, the naval aide, arrived shortly. Admiral King and General Marshall soon arrived, followed by Secretary Stimson and Secretary Knox. Later on, the other Cabinet members hurried in, likewise Senate and House leaders. The President, stunned and incredulous at first, quickly regained the poise that always marked him in moments of crisis. Closing his mind against the shock and grief of the disaster, he concentrated on plans for setting America's war effort in motion.

Neither then nor thereafter did I ever hear him mention the matter of culpability. The damage was done, and the thing to do was to repair it. Not the least of his capacity for swift and effective action was that he never complicated the task in hand by dragging in the past. At the war's end I have no doubt that he would have ordered a searching inquiry, but with

Japan at the country's throat, he regarded a "man hunt" as stupidly time-wasting.

There was a whisper at the time that his failure to put Admiral Kimmel and General Short in the prisoner's dock proceeded from his friendship for the former. It was even said that the Admiral had been the President's fishing companion and had been jumped over the heads of better men because of this personal relation. In none of it was there an atom of truth. His acquaintance with Admiral Kimmel was quite superficial, and I happen to know that the appointment was suggested by the Navy's high command.

CHAPTER XI

OPERATION *TORCH*

P EARL HARBOR HAD AN INSTANT EFFECT ON MY AU-thority as White House physician. The President felt a deep personal responsibility for every American sent abroad, and looked on any sparing of himself as little short of betrayal. Our daily schedule went by the board, and my protests were brushed aside. After December 7 about all I could do was to save as much as possible out of the wreck and watch for danger signs.

Fortunately, they were few. There was an attack of influenza in 1941, but he recovered rapidly, and regular examinations showed no cause for worry. The kidneys and liver functioned normally, the blood picture stayed on a good level, and cardiovascular measurements stayed on a good level. Nevertheless, the steady improvement that had been made in building up his muscular structure came to a standstill. Recognizing that it was likely to be a permanent condition, I cut down on his exercise as one means of conserving his strength.

Military conferences, as a matter of course, piled up on top of the heavy domestic routine. The President's assertion of his constitutional powers as commander in chief also added to strain, for it soon became the subject of bitter partisan attack. Both in Congress and out, the cry arose that he thought himself a combination of Hannibal, Napoleon, Lord Nelson, and Farragut. By way of answer, General Marshall and Admiral King have said repeatedly that the President never failed in deference to their judgment. Military decisions, however, do not stand alone but are almost invariably tied in with other considerations equally important and often more compelling. His was the ultimate responsibility, and his the position from which the picture could be viewed as a whole.

Aside from sneering at the President for his impudence in daring to assume the role of commander in chief, another favorite charge of the opposition was that he had taken advantage of the war to seize dictatorial powers. It stung him to the quick, and in one of the argumentative sessions that were a feature of White House evenings, he considered the attack in detail and at length. As he saw it, the makers of the Constitution were vigorous and explicit in defining the powers of the President. They conceived the office as the keystone in the federal arch, the one seat of administration, and the true source of the central control necessary for efficiency. Not only was the President constituted one of the three co-ordinate branches of government, with right to veto the legislative, but other high authorities were given him until the cry arose that his privileges ran far beyond those of the British Crown. Madison, Franklin, Hamilton, and their associates were not afraid of *power* because there was also responsibility to the people; their real fear was that the President had not been given sufficient strength to make him what they intended him to be— a *chief executive* in fact as well as in name.

These doubts were only with respect to the peace powers of the President, for when they came to the consideration of war powers, all conceded the necessity of *supreme control*. It was the only possible answer to the criticism that a democracy, with its balances of power, could not make war, since war called for centralized authority and instancy of decision.

"My crime," said the President at the end of his argument, "is that I have read the Constitution and stand by it. What is clearer than that the framers meant the President to be the *chief executive* in peace, and in war the *commander in chief?*"

As early as February the President threw his weight in favor of a Pacific offensive, despite the fact that Pearl Harbor had seriously depleted our naval strength. With the Japanese occupying the Admiralty Islands, New Guinea bases, Rabaul in New Britain, and preparing for the invasion of the Aleutians, he pointed out the imperative necessity of safeguarding our own shores and supply lines before turning attention to Europe. The battle of the Coral Sea was followed by Midway, and these victories ended retreat in the Pacific, and opened the way for counterblows.

In May, with Mr. Churchill a White House guest, the President put forward another bold insistence. With the Germans sweeping across the Ukraine and hammering at the gates of Moscow and Sevastopol, he argued that only some large-scale operation could avert the danger of Russia's collapse. A Channel crossing was his first thought, but when the combined Chiefs of Staff ruled that it was fantastically impossible before 1943, at the very earliest, his eyes turned to North Africa. Admitting the hazards of the invasion, he deemed it a gamble that must be taken, for Russia had to be kept in the war at whatever cost.

The long, dragging weeks of preparation for Operation *Torch* told on the President, and worse still were the anxious hours when he waited for news of the landings. Not more than 107,000 troops, mostly Americans, were in the attacking force, and before them stretched eight hundred miles of fortified coast. Holding all this vast territory was a powerful French army that still recognized the authority of Marshal Pétain. True, General Henri Giraud had cast his lot with us, and throughout the whole of North Africa numerous anti-Vichy groups were pledged to give us aid, but what the great body of Frenchmen would do was anybody's guess. If they decided to resist, it meant months of furious fighting and an estimated casualty list of sixty thousand.

Fortunately, Admiral Jean Darlan, second in command to Marshal Pétain, was found in Algiers, having come from France to the bedside of a sick son. Captured by the anti-Vichy Youth Movement, he swung to the American side after a series of complicated maneuvers engineered by General Mark Clark and Robert Murphy, and gave the order that put an end to resistance in Algiers, Oran, and Morocco. More than that, Darlan induced General Pierre Boisson to bring the whole of French West Africa into the war on the side of the Allies. Within a month French troops were fighting with us in Tunisia, a source of strength that played no small part in the crushing defeat of the Germans.

Even victory, however, brought the President no relief from strain. No sooner was the agreement with Darlan made known than a bedlam of protest broke out both in England and the United States. Members of Parliament vied with members of Congress in attacking the "shameless deal that betrayed Allied ideals," and from the safety of London General de Gaulle issued a blast against the "infamous dickering with Quislings." Even Mr. Churchill was swayed by the clamor and began to feel that a terrible blunder had been made.

General Eisenhower, through General Marshall,

rendered the President a full report, omitting no detail. General de Gaulle had not been brought into the picture because the French in North and West Africa were still bitter against him for his part in the attack on Dakar in 1940. The choice of General Giraud looked to be wise, for he was one of France's great heroes, but his authority was rejected by both naval and military commanders.

The deal with Darlan was a military necessity, and whatever the Admiral's affiliation with Vichy may have been, from the moment of his switch he had given unstinted support to Eisenhower and Clark. As a result of Darlan's co-operation we had gained a territory of 1,800,000 square miles, containing 15,000,000 inhabitants, without any large loss of life; won the assistance of French troops and ships, and "secured the opportunity to press our concentration toward the East for battle in Tunisia without worrying about the rear." After going over these reports and consulting with General Marshall, the President set his jaw and approved the Darlan-Clark agreement.

Another bedevilment that persisted throughout the whole North African venture was in connection with Spain. Not only did the President have an intense dislike for the Franco regime, but he was receiving regular reports that proved El Caudillo's sympathetic correspondence with Hitler and Mussolini. What if Franco decided to oppose our landing with his army of 150,000 in Spanish Morocco? Or if he opened his frontier for a German march across the Pyrenees that would tear through our weak flank like so much paper?

The President, however, had come to a very shrewd appreciation of Franco's strategy. According to his analysis, the savage civil struggle had left him in no shape for war, and there was the certainty that if he joined with Germany and Italy, Spain would be puppetized. As a result, while El Caudillo milked the Axis powers of all sorts of supplies under the implied promise of future co-operation, he was still sticking to his policy of nonbelligerency. The President, therefore, argued that if we could convince him that the invasion did not menace an inch of Spanish territory, Franco would keep to his shell. This proved to be the case, for Spain did not move a man against us and even went so far as to bar any German march through Spain.

Nevertheless, throughout the whole of these delicate negotiations certain groups in the United States were conducting an inflammatory campaign against Spain. Franco was damned as an active Axis partner, and a full-throated clamor insisted that the United States end immediately all diplomatic and commercial relations with Madrid. Members of Congress and great metropolitan dailies joined in the outcry, and there were those in the government only too willing to yield to the pressure. The President had to bear all this, along with the Darlan furor and the crushing anxieties of the invasion.

At the same time there were certain other momentous matters that gave him many unhappy hours. The use of poison gas was abhorrent to the President, as to every humane man, but where was there any assurance that the Germans and Japanese would not employ it? As a result, he was forced to give the Chemical Warfare Service a free hand for defensive measures, and his face never failed to sadden when the scientists reported the discovery of some new and more terrible preparation.

Even the complete success of the North African campaign and Franco's co-operative attitude brought no relief from strain. General de Gaulle continued to rampage, adding to the political chaos that followed Darlan's assassination. There was also the necessity for a quick decision as to the next military move. Regarding a conference as vital, the President arranged a meeting with Mr. Churchill and also sent a pressing invitation to Marshal Stalin. The Marshal, however, returned a somewhat curt declination. Refusing to accept North Africa as a second front, he renewed his demand for an early Channel crossing.

Casablanca was decided on as a meeting place, and in talking over the proposed journey with the President, I pointed out the dangers of air travel and the risks in a war zone. Dismissing these considerations almost irritably, he asked to be told how he stood physically. When thorough checkups showed that he suffered from nothing more than the effects of strain, the discussion ended.

CHAPTER XII

CASABLANCA

IN MIAMI, ON THE MORNING OF JANUARY 11, 1943, THE President boarded a Pan-American clipper for the flight to North Africa. Others in the party were Admiral Leahy, Harry Hopkins, Captain John McCrea, and myself. The first lap of the journey was anything but auspicious, for Admiral Leahy developed pneumonia soon after the take-off, and I deemed it wise to put him in a hospital on reaching Trinidad. His illness was a blow in more ways than one, for no man had a more intimate knowledge of French politics and politicians, and the President had counted on the Admiral as a principal adviser in a settlement of the De Gaulle–Giraud mess.

Travel, as always, bucked up the President, and my worry as to his condition was soon removed. At Bathurst, for example, where we landed after eighteen hours in the air, the rest of us were willing to rest, but not F.D.R. First touring the water front of the town in a whaleboat, he then insisted on an exploration of the lower reaches of the Gambia River.

After a grand night on board the cruiser *Memphis* we left the Clipper in Bathurst harbor and set out for the airfield where one of our C-54 land planes awaited us. The twenty-two-mile ride was over a road that jarred spines and loosened teeth, but the President took it as a great lark and laughed at our gripes.

A flight of 1,750 miles brought us to Casablanca, and I was pleased to find that a lovely villa, well south of the city, had been reserved for the President. Explosive General Patton, however, was anything but happy. "I hope you'll hurry up and get to hell out of here," he barked at our first meeting. "The Jerries occupied this place for two years, and their bombers know how to hit it. They were around ten days ago, and it's a cinch they'll be back." Fortunately, the Germans never learned about the conference until a week after we had left.

General Eisenhower, of course, was on hand, and we had our first view of him as Allied commander. A highly comforting one it was, for with all of his easy informality and lack of side, he gave a sense of force, dignity, and supreme competence. As the President watched Ike perform in meeting after meeting, pride in the wisdom of his choice was plain to see.

The conference's principal subject of discussion, naturally, was where to go from North Africa. The American position, as presented by Eisenhower and supported by the President, was for a drive into Sicily. The British viewed the operation as too hazardous and urged the selection of some more isolated spot. The debate raged rather hotly for some days, but in the end Mr. Churchill and his staff gave in.

The other matter of great importance was some resolution of the bitter differences that divided the French. Despite the fact that the troops in North Africa had not resisted the Allied landings in force, and were now fighting side by side with Americans and British in Tunisia, General de Gaulle refused to forget that they had formerly given loyalty to Pétain and the Vichy government. Thundering denunciations from London, he would take none of the olive branches held out by General Giraud, chosen to command after the assassination of Admiral Darlan.

It was not a situation that could be permitted to endure, but while De Gaulle had been told to attend the conference to discuss a solution, he chose to stay away and sulk in his tent. Even when Mr. Churchill sent him sharp messages, emphasizing the fact that the whole Free French movement depended entirely on British money and support, he did not arrive until the eighth day. Moreover, although he landed early in the morning, it was not until late afternoon that he chose to make himself available. One of the Prime Minister's bons mots that went the rounds ran like this: "De Gaulle? Oh, we call him Joan of Arc and hope for some bishops to burn him."

Kenneth Pendar, our vice-consul in Marrakech, also stresses General de Gaulle's egotism in his informative book, *Adventure in Diplomacy*. According to him, the following conversation took place after the General's arrival in Casablanca:

President Roosevelt told De Gaulle that France was in such military straits that she needed a general of Napoleonic caliber. *"Mais, je suis cet homme,"* said De Gaulle. She was, went on the President, in such a bad financial shape that she also needed a Colbert. *"Mais,"* said De Gaulle simply, *"je suis cet homme."* Finally, said the President, controlling his amazement, she was so devitalized politically that she needed a Clemenceau. De Gaulle drew himself up with dignity, and said, *"Mais, je suis cet homme."* It was this interview that made the President realize the full extent of the psychological problem De Gaulle presented.*

I myself did not hear of any such parley, but Pendar insists that he had it from a "high authority." From what we saw of the General, I am disposed to believe it.

Any lingering doubts as to the President's fitness were removed by the way he handled himself in the trying negotiations that followed De Gaulle's arrival. Argument is a weary business, especially when edged by irritation, but never once did he lose his reasonableness or show impatience with what could only be termed downright bullheadedness. The Prime Minister reached the explosion point on several occasions, and it

---

* From *Adventures in Diplomacy* by Kenneth Pendar. Copyright, 1945, by Kenneth Pendar. Reprinted by permission of Dodd, Mead & Co.

was entirely as a result of the President's efforts that the closing day saw General de Gaulle and General Giraud shake hands in public and announce agreement on a plan of co-operation. That the agreement was breached at a later date, De Gaulle pushing Giraud completely out of the picture, does not take away from the value of the accomplishment.

The ten days at Casablanca were so packed with the drudgery of continual conferences that only on two occasions did the President have any respite. One night the Sultan of Morocco came to dinner, bringing with him his Grand Vizier and the Crown Prince, and bearing as a gift one of the most beautiful gold-mounted daggers I have ever seen. Gorgeously attired in white silk robes and gleaming with jewels, he proved an interesting table companion. The President, fortunately, had made inquiries as to the Sultan's tastes and habits, and care was taken not to serve either alcohol or pork products.

Gossip about what went on at the dinner upset the French authorities considerably. The President, with his usual eager interest in people, made the condition of the Sultan's subjects a principal topic of discussion, advising irrigation, development of water power, social reforms, and heaven knows what else. The French, as the governing power, were quite agitated at the thought of a New Deal in Morocco, but F.D.R. contended that he deserved their thanks for his intelligent suggestions.

152

The other break in the drudgery of conferences came on a Thursday while General de Gaulle's arrival was being awaited. Deciding to spend a day with our troops, the President drafted General Patton as his guide. Starting early in the morning, we changed to jeeps after an eighty-five-mile drive and inspected the Second Armored Division and the Third Infantry Division. At first the men could not believe that it was really the President, and then it was thrilling to see their faces light up and hear their cheers.

At noon we left the highway and sat down to a fine meal provided by an Army field kitchen. Boiled ham, sweet potatoes, string beans, bread, butter, jam, and coffee. A great lover of picnics, the President ate heartily and only lamented the lack of a "hot dog." After luncheon there came the inspection of the Ninth Division and then a visit to two cemeteries where wreaths were laid on the graves of American boys.

Even more than our own troops, a certain Frenchman will always remember the occasion as a day of days. The baker from Rabat happened to be delivering fresh bread at the time of the inspection, and the President called him up to the jeep for a handshake and a few words in French. According to Kenneth Pendar's later report, it made the baker's fortune, for the entire population of Rabat poured into his shop for weeks, fighting to touch the fingers that had clasped the hand of Franklin D. Roosevelt.

A cold rain beat down on us all the way back to

Casablanca, but after a day in a jeep, covering more than two hundred miles, the President was as brisk as when he started. All the same, I insisted on a quiet dinner and sent him to bed at 9:30 for the first long night of rest since arriving in North Africa. Mr. Churchill, considerate enough in everything else, had been proceeding on his favorite assumption that midnight was "just the shank of the evening."

At noon on Sunday, after a press conference, much posing for pictures, and many farewells, our party joined that of the Prime Minister for a motor cavalcade to Marrakech, an old Berber and Arab town some 150 miles to the south. We reached there just before sunset and found that Vice Consul Pendar had made elaborate preparations for our care and comfort. La Saadia, the villa assigned to us for the night, had been remodeled by the late Moses Taylor, an American millionaire, and was something that might have been conjured up by a rub of Aladdin's lamp. Formerly an olive grove, the grounds had been turned into a fairyland by fountains, waterfalls, and every variety of tree and flower. The villa itself was also out of the Arabian Nights, for the rooms were ankle deep in priceless rugs, and each had a bath of black onyx tile large enough for an elephant herd.

The great feature of La Saadia was a sloping tower six stories high, and after hearing Mr. Churchill rave over the view, the President determined to see it for himself. The stairs were too narrow for his chair, so he laughingly called for volunteers. George Fox and Mike Reilly, head of the Secret Service detail, came forward, and making a cradle of their hands, carried him to the topmost terrace, where he sat for half an hour, fascinated by the kaleidoscopic play of color on the massive peaks of the Grand Atlas range.

The real purpose of the Marrakech stop was to put the Casablanca agreements in final form, and although the job was started directly after dinner, work continued until half past three. When it came to speed and precision in dictating, I could note little difference between the President and the Prime Minister, but it pleased me to note that our man seemed the fresher of the two at the finish, and that without stimulants.

We left Marrakech promptly at 7:30 the next morning, and Mr. Churchill proved his affection by getting up to see us off. With his usual disregard for the conventions, he wore a noisy dressing gown over his "siren suit," had his head covered by an air marshal's cap and his feet stuck into black velvet slippers with his initials embroidered on the toes. The photographers begged for a shot but backed off when the Prime Minister jovially threatened them with his big black cigar.

Any hope that I may have had for a leisurely, restful homeward trip was soon dispelled. On reaching Bathurst the President dragged us off for an inspection of the *Aimwell,* a 560-ton seagoing tug that we had built for the British under Lend-Lease. This done, he

spent the rest of the day sight-seeing with Lord Swin-
ton, governor of the British provinces of West Africa,
who had flown over from Nigeria. As in the case of
the Sultan of Morocco, the President gave Lord Swin-
ton an earful, telling him flatly that wise administration
commanded that more attention be given to the health
and well-being of the native population. Shocked by
the evidences of poverty, and particularly by the sweep
of disease, he described the work being done by the
Navy epidemiological teams in the Pacific and urged
that the British take advantage of our discoveries and
methods.

Conferences took up the night, but at six o'clock
the next morning the President hurried us off for a
690-mile flight to Liberia. There we sweltered through
a luncheon given in honor of F.D.R. and President
Barclay by Major General Fitzgerald, commander of
American troops in Liberia. That ordeal endured, we
then marched out into the burning sun for a review
of the American Liberian army. As if that were not
punishment enough, the President insisted on visiting
a Firestone rubber plantation, optimistically described
as a "small tract," but actually covering twenty-five
square miles. He found it intensely interesting, keeping
up a continual fire of questions, but the rest of us,
dripping sweat from every pore, cursed each separate
tree. Back in Bathurst that evening, we had a delightful dinner on board the *Memphis* and took off at eleven
o'clock for the flight to Brazil.

In Natal we breakfasted with Admiral Ingram on the *Black Hawk,* and at ten o'clock President Vargas came on board for a conference that lasted well into the afternoon. On arrival at the airport for the last leg of our long journey, officers of Military Intelligence rushed up with the alarming report that an attack was to be made on the President's plane some time after the take-off. Brazil, they pointed out, was still full of Germans, and only a short time before, a large transport plane had mysteriously burst into flame over British Guiana, killing all of the occupants. The President, however, refused to delay his departure, accepting danger as something to be expected.

At Trinidad after a 2,200-mile hop, we stopped for a survey of the Army installations made as a result of the deal that gave us bases in return for the fifty destroyers. The President made no secret of his pride in the vast development, and certainly it was his right, for when war came it was from Trinidad that we shuttled our planes all over Europe, Asia, and Africa. Picking up Admiral Leahy, now fully recovered from his attack of pneumonia, we headed for home in the early morning.

The President's birthday—January 30—found us over Haiti. As we ate a festal luncheon in honor of the occasion, the pilot circled low, and Mr. Roosevelt recalled his tour of the island in 1916, pointing out the mountain trails climbed on the hard journey from Port au Prince to Cap Haitien. As he reminisced of those days when none had been more swift or strong, there must have been an ache of heart, yet no shadow of it could be detected in eyes or voice.

The Casablanca journey was very helpful to me, as I was able to inspect many of the Navy medical hospitals in North Africa.

CHAPTER XIII

TEHERAN

THE MONTHS THAT FOLLOWED CASABLANCA WERE wearing, but Allied successes lessened the nervous strain, and the President not only picked up weight but lost some of his care lines. He had made a swing around the country in 1942, inspecting encampments and war plants, and now in April he decided on another inspection tour, and also an exchange of visits with Manuel Avila Camacho, president of Mexico. With his own eyes he wanted to see the progress of the production that would make America "the arsenal of democracy," and it was imperative that the closest possible relations be established with our sister republic on the south.

The President's seemingly inexhaustible energy had never ceased to amaze me, but this 1943 trip of 7,243 miles, a "mere jaunt" as he termed it, proved a new high in incessant activity. Twenty states were covered, and there was nothing perfunctory about the inspection. He insisted on seeing every phase of troop training and spent hours in the factories, grasping the intricacies of plane construction and having workers explain the new weapons with which he was not familiar. A particular fascination was the bazooka, a plain piece of iron pipe that fired a rocket-like missile capable of piercing two-inch armor plate. Not only did he go over it in careful detail but demanded a demonstration.

Nothing seemed to tire him, not even the constant speeches, for whether in a camp or a factory, cheering soldiers and workers wanted to hear his voice. There were also the crowds that greeted him in every city, for even though no paper ever mentioned his arrival or departure, the news spread by grapevine. At Evansville, Indiana, a member of our party came in from the station platform laughing his head off. "There's a five-year-old girl out there," he told the President, "who's making quite a riot. She says she doesn't care if you are a military secret, she wants to see you."

For everybody except the President the Mexican interlude was a good deal of a nightmare. The ride across the desert was hot and dusty, and at Monterrey the crowds were unmanageable, breaking through the line of march time and again, driving the Secret Service detail almost insane. The banquet and the speeches stretched out for years, but the President beamed through it all, happy as a bluebird over the proof that his "Good Neighbor" policy was more than a political slogan.

Although Mr. Churchill had been a White House

guest in May, another meeting became imperative when Mussolini fled Rome in July. Quebec was chosen, with August 16 as the date; and every effort was made to have Marshal Stalin attend. He refused, however, just as he had rejected the Casablanca invitation; and Mr. Churchill gave it as his opinion that "Uncle Joe" could never be induced to leave the safety of his own domain.

Although the Quebec conferences were almost continuous, there was no sense of pressure. Having spent so many summers at Campobello, the President knew Canada and Canadians, and he and MacKenzie King had been friends since their Harvard days. From the very first there was a friendliness that made for understandings and agreements; and many important decisions, particularly those relating to over-all commands in the various areas, were reached without irritated debate.

The President was in rare form throughout the week, and good news from the Pacific lifted his spirits higher and higher. The victories in the Aleutians and at Tarawa were like wine to him, and all of his speeches rang with confidence and challenge. The one that I remember best was where he gave this perfect expression of his philosophy of life:

I am everlasting angry only at those who assert vociferously that the Four Freedoms and the Atlantic Charter are nonsense because they are unattainable. If those people had lived a century and a half ago they would have sneered and said that the Declaration of Independence was utter piffle. If they had lived nearly a thousand years ago they would have laughed uproariously at the ideals of Magna Charta. And if they had lived several thousand years ago, they would have derided Moses when he came down from the mountain with the Ten Commandments. We concede that these great teachings are not perfectly lived up to today. *But I would rather be a builder than a wrecker, hoping always that the structure of life is growing, not dying.*

As summer gave way to fall, the conviction grew that long-distance dealings with Marshal Stalin could not possibly meet Allied needs. While Russia was now holding the offensive and increasingly aided by the delivery of supplies from the United States and Great Britain, Moscow screamed louder than ever for a second front. The President discounted the rumors of a separate peace between Russia and Germany; nevertheless he was worried by Marshal Stalin's increasing irritation and his refusals of all requests for closer co-operation. No military observer from either England or America was permitted to visit the Russian front, and Russia's battle plans were shrouded in darkest secrecy.

From the President's point of view, it was even more vital that Stalin should commit himself to postwar co-operation with the Allies, joining wholeheartedly in the organization of the United Nations. Just as he had no doubt of ultimate victory, so was he equally convinced that Russia, emerging from the war as a world power, would be the key to world peace.

There was also the problem of China and her 400,000,000 starving people, keeping up the war against Japan by sheer courage and indomitable spirit. Chiang Kai-shek not only begged for improvements in the air transport system but insisted on a compaign to reopen the Burma road. All of these matters could only be ironed out by face to face conferences; and when the President communicated with Prime Minister Churchill, it was agreed that a meeting must be arranged.

Marshal Stalin, duly approached, expressed a willingness to go as far away from Moscow as Teheran and refused to accept Basra as an alternative even when Teheran's inaccessibility was pointed out to him. In view of the desperateness of the situation the President yielded; and Chiang Kai-shek, without demur, agreed to fly to Cairo for a conference in advance of Teheran.

This time my one insistence was on a more leisurely manner of travel, for I knew that the journey to Teheran would be far more arduous than the Casablanca trip. The President agreed, and instead of flying across the Atlantic we boarded the dreadnought *Iowa*, giving him a week of needed rest at sea. Antisubmarine screening destroyers went along, the first of many precautions, for every mile of the way to Teheran entailed grave danger. German U-boats ranged the

Atlantic and the Mediterranean, and beyond Gibraltar there was the peril of enemy planes and the destructive glider bomb.

Our party disembarked at Oran, Algeria, early on the morning of November 20 and were met at the quay by General Eisenhower. This was something that had been strongly opposed by the Secret Service, the reason being that the General's presence would reveal that some particularly distinguished passenger was landing and put the President in danger. Also it would mess up their security arrangements for the trip from the dock to the airdrome. F.D.R. hit the ceiling when he heard of it, and sent word for Ike to meet him without fail.

The General boarded our plane for the flight to Tunis and on arrival naturally assumed that the President would want to proceed immediately to his villa for a rest. Instead of that F.D.R. insisted on a tour of old Carthage, and then after two hours with the mail that was waiting for him, he bundled Ike into a jeep and hurried off for an inspection of Colonel Elliott Roosevelt's air squadron.

General Eisenhower and a lot of other brass, both British and American, dined with the President, but he alone was kept for conference. When I went in to give my patient the usual look-see at bedtime, he confided to me that a main purpose of his Tunis stop was to make up his mind as to Eisenhower's capacity for the high post of Supreme Allied Commander.

He was delighted with the calm assurance displayed by Eisenhower. With the Sicilian and Salerno campaigns under his belt, there could be no question of his fitness as an over-all leader.

This was a surprise, for it had been common gossip before we left Washington that General Marshall would have the job, turning over his post of Chief of Staff to Eisenhower. This idea, however, the President explained, had been abandoned as a result of Marshall's strong dissent. The exchange, he pointed out, would simply mean that both men would waste valuable time learning their way around in a brand-new job. It was much better, the General insisted, to let him stay where he was, and in the same breath he urged Eisenhower as one brilliantly qualified to take the over-all command.

Restored to full vigor by the sea voyage and in fine spirits, the President spent Sunday on a tour of the battlefields. General Eisenhower, acting as guide, described how the Allied break-through, first at Medjez el Bab and then at Tebourba, brought about an almost immediate German collapse and gave us control of the entire area. That night we boarded the plane for the 1,851-mile hop to Cairo, but even darkness did not remove the danger from German planes; so we flew inland instead of following the coast. As a result, dawn found us looking down on the Nile some 150 miles above Cairo, and with no sign of the fighter escort that was to have met us for the daylight jaunt.

As we learned later, the commander of the squadron had confused local time with Greenwich mean time, a difference of two hours. Luckily, no enemies were encountered, and on nearing Cairo Major Otis Bryan, copilot of the plane, made several "off course" circles to give the President a good view of the Pyramids.

I had looked forward to our stay in the Egyptian capital with considerable unease, having heard some disturbing reports about health conditions. A main worry was a very prevalent disease known as "jyppy tummy," a complaint with dysentery symptoms. Ambassador Kirk, however, turned his villa over to the President, with all of its modern conveniences; and as always, we carried our own water, milk, and cream. Consequently not a single upset was suffered by any of our party, while Mr. Churchill, less careful, had a bad time of it with "jyppy tummy."

All of the sessions were held in the villa, another protection for the President; and, aside from a visit to the Sphinx and the Pyramids with the Prime Minister, he was also barred from sight-seeing tours. This ruling brought some vigorous protests, but the military authorities stood firm, pointing out that the villa was only five hundred miles from the nearest German bombing base. Why no attack was made during our Cairo stay can only be explained by the failure of the German Intelligence staff to function properly.

By this time the Prime Minister was a familiar sight to most of us, and everybody, quite openly, looked forward with curiosity to seeing Chiang Kai-shek. The President, as I knew from several conversations, had doubts about him as a result of conflicting reports; but they were removed after the very first meeting. The Generalissimo's courage, statesmanship, and patriotism made a profound impression, and it was with real Western frankness that he laid all of his cards on the table. Later in the week, during one of our bedtime chats, the President made no secret of his conviction that Chiang was the one great hope for China's unification and upward climb to modernization. Moreover, he was the only man who could keep China firm against Japan.

The plenary sessions, presided over by the President, the Prime Minister, and the Generalissimo and attended by the combined Chiefs of Staff, worked out military problems in detail and then gave Chiang Kai-shek the assurances that he asked. Manchuria, Formosa, and the Pescadores were to be returned to China; and Korea, in due course, was to become free and independent. To these promises the honor of Great Britain and the United States was pledged.

The Cairo conference, while important, was a curtain raiser for the drama of Teheran, where the President of the United States was to come face to face with the unquestioned ruler of the vast Soviet Union. We left the Egyptian capital on a Saturday morning, and all of us were thrilled that our direct route carried us over the Holy Land and the historic basins of the

Euphrates and Tigris. The Casablanca flight had bored the President, for he missed seeing towns and people, but now the pilot flew low, and we looked down on Bethlehem, Jerusalem, Jericho, the Jordan, and the Dead Sea, and after dreary travel over the wastes of Iraq, circled several times over fabulous Bagdad.

Later on, our flight presented some very real problems, for Teheran lies deep in a bowl, surrounded by mountains with altitudes varying from ten to fifteen thousand feet. Soaring over mighty peaks and then worming a way through narrow passes provided a series of spectacular contrasts, but the President loved every minute of it. It was not that he did not realize danger, but simply that his mind was never open to apprehensions.

We glided down through the sunshine of afternoon to the City of the Peacock Throne; and as security reasons made an official reception inadvisable, we were able to drive quietly and quickly to the American Legation. I was quartered in the compound of Major General Donald H. Connolly, head of our Persian Gulf Service Command, along with others; but just as I was getting ready for bed that night, a telephone call ordered all of us to report at once to the Legation.

On arrival we found that Marshal Stalin had just sent word that the President *must* switch from the Legation to a palace in the Russian compound. His Secret Service, it developed, had unearthed a conspiracy to assassinate the Marshal, the Prime Minister,

168

or the President, or maybe all three. F.D.R. was disposed to refuse at first but agreed when it was explained to him that Teheran had been under complete German control only a few months before, and that the city was still filled with Axis sympathizers.

The move was made next day; and from a security standpoint, nothing could have been more desirable. The British Legation stood next door to the Marshal's compound, and four entire blocks were screened off, with no travel permitted and guns and guards every few feet. As a home, however, the palace was impossible. Even after a sanitary squad had cleaned up and bedding had been brought in, we faced the difficulty of giving a formal dinner that night without a kitchen, cooking utensils, or dishes. General Connolly, our good angel, came to the rescue by sending over a crew with field kitchens and foodstuffs, and, fortunately, we had brought along our Filipino mess boys from the ship.

Meeting Marshal Stalin, of course, was the big thrill. On the voyage over, there had been a lot of discussion both about the man and his form of government, and most of us down in the lower levels held to the opinion that there was little likelihood of bridging the gulf between Communism and our own free way of life. The President did not share these fears, insisting that the Marxian philosophy did not have, and could not possibly have, any lasting appeal either to the minds or to the souls of men.

169

For one thing, it was a program of unrelieved materialism, utterly ignoring every spiritual value. Nothing, he claimed, was ever more true than that man did not live by bread alone. Communism's denial of God, the emphasis on hate, and its refusal to admit the dignity of man, were some of the reasons he advanced for the philosophy's inevitable failure. Even in Russia, he pointed out, Communism retained power only through armed force, never-ending purges, and the suppression of free speech, free press, and free assembly. And at that, Stalin had been forced to depart radically from many tenets of Communist faith, restoring the unequal wage and the incentive motive. It was much more probable, in his opinion, that the Russians would swing to a perfervid nationalism, and revert to the imperialism of the czars.

The President had read everything about Stalin that he could lay his hands on, and thought that the Marshal's life story gave a good many answers to the riddle of the man. First, he was a Georgian, not a Russian, and therefore an Oriental. His young manhood had been given over to robbery and murder, all justified by the Marxian theory that the end justified the means. Forced into dictatorship by the struggle for power, like every dictator he was steeped in distrust of everything and everybody. Worst of all, he was a provincial who had never been outside of his own country.

"Breaking down these habits of life," said the President, "is going to be a hard job, but I bank on his realism. He must be tired of sitting on bayonets, just as he must realize that the war is bound to break down his iron curtain, letting his millions see the higher living standards of other peoples. If I can convince him that our offer of co-operation is on the square, and that we want to be comrades rather than enemies, I'm betting that he'll come in. And," the President added with a grin, "what helps a lot is that Stalin is the only man I have to convince. Joe doesn't worry about a Congress or a Parliament. He's the whole works."

The Marshal's appearance came as a surprise, for we had pictured him as a big man. Instead of that he was below average height. While courteous enough at the first meeting, his cordiality wasn't anything you could warm your hands by, and some of us had a sneaking idea that the President had his work cut out for him. It was plain to see that he had just as much curiosity about F.D.R. as the President had about him. All through the initial visits his sharp eyes never quit probing.

The results of the conference are now history, written large for all men to see and judge. Without passing on them, I can say that the decisions were due in large measure to the President's superb handling of a delicate situation. Marshal Stalin, invincibly suspicious, also looked at everything from the standpoint of Russia's interests. While Mr. Churchill had more breadth and elasticity, each proposition was measured with relation to the vital concerns of the British Empire. Both being strong-willed, outspoken men, clashes were inevitable, and old bitternesses added to irritation. The Marshal could not forget Mr. Churchill's earlier denunciations of Russia and its form of government and shot home many a barbed remark. The Prime Minister, unchanged in his dislike of Communism, gave back as good as he got. It was the President, standing between, untiring and undiscouraged, who reconciled differences and found bases of agreement.

Stalin insisted that the Allies attack in the west in force and at the earliest possible moment. What he demanded was a mighty blow straight at the heart of France, and one that would carry on into Germany. Mr. Churchill held stubbornly to his contention that the drive should be launched from Mediterranean bases against what he termed the "soft underbelly of the Axis." The President sided with the Marshal and finally swung the Prime Minister into line.

There was, however, a condition. What he asked and demanded from Stalin in return was this pledge: "We shall seek the co-operation and the active participation of all nations, large and small, whose peoples in heart and mind are dedicated, as are our own peoples, to the elimination of tyranny and slavery, oppression and intolerance. We will welcome them, as they choose to come, into a world family of democratic nations." Moreover, and this is particularly significant in the light of recent events, he secured Stalin's agreement to a three-power pact that guaranteed Iran's "territorial integrity, sovereignty, and political independence."

At the outset, the Marshal had been taciturn and withdrawn, but toward the last he opened up considerably and even showed a sense of humor. After a dinner session that had lasted until eleven o'clock, the President went to his room, and I persuaded him to stay put. Going back, I explained to the Marshal that Mr. Roosevelt had retired but would be available at ten the next morning. Getting up, he cocked an eye at the Prime Minister and dryly remarked, "Well, I'm glad that there is somebody here who knows when it is time to go home."

Nothing, however, showed the change in Marshal Stalin's whole attitude more clearly than the short speech he made at a party in honor of Mr. Churchill's sixty-ninth birthday. For the first time he made public acknowledgment of Russia's debt to the United States, and also, for the first time, he put by his suspiciousness, and talked in terms of fairly generous comradeship. Here is the stenographic record of his remarks as translated:

I want to tell you, from the Russian point of view, what the President and the United States have done to win the war. The most important things in this war are machines. The United States has proved that it can turn out from eight to ten thousand airplanes a month. Russia can only turn out, at most, three thousand airplanes a month. England turns out three thousand to thirty-five hundred which are principally heavy bombers. The United States, therefore, is a country of machines. Without the use of those machines, through Lend-Lease, we would lose this war.

CHAPTER XIV

TEHERAN AFTERMATH

IN A RECENT INTERVIEW, GIVEN IN SHANGHAI, MME
Chiang Kai-shek was quoted as having been
"shocked" by the President's looks during the Cairo
conferences. She thought that he had "fallen off considerably," and seemed "quite ill." Mr. Churchill is
also reported to have said that he noted signs of deterioration in the President at Teheran, although I
have never been able to find any direct statement.

It was fortunate for the Madame that I did not share
her opinion, or else I would have clamped down on
the luncheons, dinners, and conferences to which she
and the Generalissimo were bidden by the President.
As it was, I saw no reason to limit the President's activities in Cairo, even though many of the sessions
with the Chinese were long and tiring. As for Mr.
Churchill's alleged statement, I insist that every fact
in the case refutes it. The days and nights of argument
wearied the President, to be sure, but my examinations
at the close of the conference found him so fit, both
mentally and physically, that I did not think it neces-

sary to urge any change in the exacting itinerary that had been mapped out.

After farewells, we left Teheran for a night in the high hills with Major General Donald Connolly and his men. A hard trip, but the President insisted that a visit was the least possible tribute that could be paid to a gallant officer and his equally gallant troops. In his opinion, Russia's successful resistance to the German drive was almost entirely due to Connolly's Persian Gulf Command, a force that never numbered more than 29,000. Building and operating a railroad and truck line from the Persian Gulf to the Caspian Sea, this unbeatable bunch of Americans carried every known kind of war material across burning deserts and over mountains as formidable as our own Rockies.

Every mile of the way was a battle, not only against the elements and the ghastly terrain but against the brigands who swooped down from the heights in foray after foray. Virtually isolated, they had also the problem of subsistence, and hunting parties had to go out regularly for the bear and deer that offered the only supply of fresh meat. The President's visit was the one lift in years of danger and drudgery, and General Connolly's gratitude was actually pathetic.

We flew to Cairo on the following day, and a first order of business was a conference with the President of Turkey. F.D.R.'s own plane was sent to Agra, and on İsmet İnönü's arrival the two went into an immediate huddle. As I learned later, it had no concrete results. Turkey wanted a guarantee of territorial integrity as her price for entering the war against Germany, and Russia was not disposed to give it. Nevertheless, İsmet İnönü agreed to maintain his neutrality, scrupulously denying aid and comfort to the Axis powers.

After that came three crowded days given over to discussions with the combined Chiefs of Staff. The Teheran decisions were reviewed, plans laid down for the war in the Mediterranean, and the selection of General Eisenhower as Supreme Commander definitely confirmed. The British might have had a desire to land the top job for one of their own, but the President's insistence, backed up by convincing proofs of Ike's competence as a soldier, strategist, and administrator, resulted in his unanimous choice.

On boarding the plane for the flight from Cairo to Tunis, the President calmly announced that he wanted to fly low over El Alamein, Tobruk, Bengazi, and Sfax. A dangerous business even with fighter escort, for the Germans still maintained active airfields on Crete, no more than two hundred miles from Tobruk, but he could not be dissuaded. All morning we skimmed over the scenes of Montgomery's stand and Rommel's rout, but while the rest of us scanned the skies for German planes, the President had eyes only for the battlefields. After luncheon, to everybody's relief, he decided on a nap, and we took advantage of it to steer a swift, straight course for Tunis.

The new Supreme Commander met us at the airport, and after a night in his villa, we took off for Malta, although with some shaking of heads. Ike worried about German fighters still based in Italy, and I stewed over the prospect of another fatiguing day for the President. Luckily, no enemy planes were encountered, but as we came down at Malta it was discovered that the landing flaps were out of commission. Great commotion, but F.D.R. never turned a hair. "Fine," he said. "Here's where we see just how good our pilots are." Major Bryan, praise be, lived up to the best traditions of the air service, for he landed us with a skill that brought a permanent grin to the face of General Spaatz.

The day, as I had feared, was a trying one for the President, both physically and emotionally. For long, terrible months the Maltese had withstood daily bombardment and every horror of battle and famine; and as we rode over the island in jeeps, it was through a nightmare of ruin. The President, in a moving speech, presented a citation to the citizens as a token of America's admiration for their indomitable defense, and men and women wept as they cheered.

Malta did not finish the day by any means, for we flew to Sicily after luncheon. There the "failing" President reviewed troops, riding up and down the ranks in a bumpy jeep, decorated Lieutenant General Mark Clark and other heroes of the Italian campaign, and then held conferences with Eisenhower and others of the high command. General George Patton was among them, rather subdued as an aftermath of the slapping incident, but F.D.R. made no reference to it whatsoever.

At the time the story broke in Washington, the President had been deeply disturbed but accepted General Eisenhower's judgment that Patton was too valuable to be relieved as a result of his momentary attack of nerves. "Old Blood and Guts" had been the real spearhead of the Sicilian campaign and stood out above all others as the best man to carry the ball in a broken field.

Only heavy weather and Ike's vigorous protests kept the President from flying over Naples after the review. More conferences filled the evening in Tunis, and at 6:30 the next morning we took off for the 2,500-mile nonstop flight to Dakar. A rough trip, for storms blew up, and there were hours when we flew blind through dense fog, but the President bore thunderheads and strain without a symptom of discomfort. More conferences at Dakar, and in the evening a French gunboat sneaked us out of the harbor to the battleship *Iowa*, which was waiting outside.

During the voyage home the President addressed the crew on December 16, 1943. Since these remarks would never be published, being highly informal, it seems to me that the following paragraph is a very excellent commentary on the sincerity of President Roosevelt in his work with Churchill and Stalin.

One of the reasons I went abroad, as you know, was to try by conversations with other nations, to see that this war that we are all engaged in shall not happen again. We have an idea—all of us, I think—that hereafter we have got to eliminate from the human race nations like Germany and Japan; eliminate them from the possibility of ruining the lives of a whole lot of other nations, and in these talks in North Africa, Egypt, and Persia, with the Chinese, the Russians, the Turks, and others, we made real progress. Obviously it will be necessary when we win the war to make the possibility of a future upsetting of our civilization an impossible thing. I don't say forever. None of us can look that far ahead. But I do say as long as any Americans and others who are alive today are still alive. That objective is worth fighting for. It is a part of democracy which exists in most of the world. At Upper Teheran, where the Prime Minister, Marshal Stalin, and I met, in one sense it followed that as heads of governments we were representing between two-thirds and three-fourths of the entire population of the world. We all had the same fundamental aims—stopping what has been going on in the past four years, and that is why I believe from the point of view of people—just plain people —this trip has been worthwhile.

A strenuous five weeks, but the sea trip erased the President's fatigue lines and put him back in good shape. At a press conference on the afternoon of his return from a trip covering 17,742 sea, air, and land miles, the correspondents all agreed that he "looked in the pink."

The domestic situation, however, made new and

180

heavier demands on his strength. Not only was there the threat of a nation-wide railroad strike, but the steel workers were on the edge of a walkout that would have paralyzed production. Moving decisively, the President took over the railroads by proclamation and intervened successfully in the steel dispute. No man had greater sympathy with the aspirations of labor, but he held unshakably to the conviction that strikes in wartime came dangerously close to sabotage.

At this time, too, a peculiarly painful matter was put up to him for decision. From London came word that German laboratories had gone far in developing the possibilities of bacterial warfare, and were on the eve of loading rocket planes with toxic agents that would spread death and disease—germs of every kind, in fact, deadly alike to human beings, animals, and plant life. The President refused to credit it at first, but the British, frantically alarmed, forced him to a choice. Were we to take the chance that there was no truth in the rumor, or would we adopt defensive and offensive measures of our own?

The decision tormented the President for days, and he yielded to the Army and the Navy only when assured that research was bound to result in important peacetime benefits, such as the cure for many deadly diseases or else immunization against them. Straightway George W. Merck, the distinguished chemist, was called in as a Special Assistant to the Secretary of War, and assigned to the Chemical Warfare Service. The

181

Navy, as its own special project, set up Medical Research Unit No. 1, and we worked in closest co-operation with Mr. Merck. The weapons developed were and are, in my opinion, more terrible and devastating than the atomic bomb. Along with bacteria, fungi, viruses, etc., the vibration of noise was also studied, opening a new and limitless field.

I do not think there was a time throughout the war when the President ceased to pray that the day would never come when we would have to resort to a method of warfare more frightful than any ever devised by the mind of man. Before his death, thank God, we were able to keep our promise that out of horror would come good. An effective drug has been discovered for the treatment of trachoma, also a remedy for heavy metal poisons, a weed killer, and a vaccine for the control of rinderpest, that terrible cattle disease. Best news of all, cancer research has been greatly advanced.

As always, the President went to Hyde Park for Christmas, but problems followed him, and just to make things worse, he had the bad luck to contract influenza. The attack hung on and finally left behind a nagging inflammation of the bronchial tubes. Coughing spells racked him by day and broke his rest at night. More disturbing than anything else, there was the definite loss of his usual ability to come back quickly.

Even so, nothing could induce him to slow down, for his mind had locked on legislation that he deemed vital to the prosecution of the war. What he framed and urged was a national service law that would draft all able-bodied men and women for essential industry, with certain exceptions, and a realistic tax law to absorb unreasonable individual and corporate profits. What with bronchitis, and his belief in the bills as both just and imperative, Congressional opposition shook him loose from his usual serene balance. The soldiers' vote measure was denounced as a fraud, and in his veto of the tax bill he stigmatized it as "relief not for the needy but for the greedy."

So it went on; one day up and one day down. His heart, of course, became a subject of concern because of his continual coughing, and in order to lessen the load on it, we decided to institute a gradual reduction in diet that would lower his weight by ten pounds. The problem now was to protect the President's reserve strength, with constant watch on the heart, and this became the particular business of Commander Howard Bruenn. Let me say, parenthetically, that the supervisory care of this young doctor would have added years to the patient's life but for the sudden and unforeseen cerebral hemorrhage. Proof is furnished by the fact that the President's heart functioned strongly to the very last.

When the racking cough persisted, I decided on a full-dress examination, and in addition to Navy personnel, called in Dr. James E. Paullin of Atlanta and Dr. Paul Dickens, clinical professor of medicine at

183

George Washington University. The result showed a moderate degree of arteriosclerosis, although no more than normal in a man of his age; some changes in the cardiographic tracing; cloudiness in his sinuses; and bronchial irritation. It was the judgment of all that the President should take a vacation in the South and, particularly, that he quit smoking to get rid of the sinus and throat trouble.

Several press conferences were canceled during this period, and the White House press room began to buzz with conjectures as to the state of the President's health. Rumors also started to spread; and to meet the situation, Steve Early asked me to meet with the correspondents and talk frankly. I thought the suggestion a good one and in answer to questions gave these statements:

I have been completely responsible for holding up the President these last three or four days. The bronchitis has made him a little hoarse, and I felt that if we could keep him in his study for his work, and not run him from room to room with changes of temperature, we could clear this thing up. I can say to you that the checkup is satisfactory. When we got through we decided that for a man of sixty-two we had very little to argue about, with the exception that we have had to combat the influenza plus the respiratory complications that came along afterward.

The only thing we need to finish up on is just the residuals of this bronchitis and one of his sinuses, and they are clearing rapidly. He is feeling quite well this morning. In fact, I think he will be getting up today. The greatest criticism we can have is that we have not been able to provide him with enough exercise and sunshine. That is something we have lacked right along in the press of things. We weighed him ten days ago, and he was 187 and a fraction. But we have him on a pretty good regime now, and have decreased his food just a little. Yesterday he weighed 183½.

Where to go for rest and sun was soon settled by Bernie Baruch's offer of his South Carolina plantation as a quiet retreat. We left Washington on April 8, and the month of quiet and rest accomplished all I had hoped. While the President kept in close touch with his secretariat and the heads of the armed forces, visitors were barred and paper work cut down to a minimum. Improvement began at once, for on April 18 an examination developed these findings:

"Still some mucous drainage from his sinuses; blood pressure dropping down; very interesting fact that the readings are lower in the evening than in the morning; moreover, posture seems to have a great deal to do with fluctuations in the systolic pressure."

On April 23 a consultation decided that the President could now go on a set schedule that would include moderate exercise. His diet was so organized that while the caloric value would be high, it would contain very little irritating substances for the intestines. A certain amount of trouble with gas formation continued, but these symptoms were completely clear by May 1, and the report on that day was satisfactory:

"Patient free from abdominal distress; feels very well subjectively, and is in grand shape objectively."

The examination also showed that his blood pressure was within normal range; that there were no cardiac symptoms, and kidney and liver functions both normal. In the week before our return to Washington, his cough had cleared up entirely, and he was out on the water every day, handling a rod and tackle with all of his old strength. Here, as proof, are the results of a physical examination made on May 10, 1944:

Temperature: 98.6

Pulse: 72

Respiration: 20

General Appearance: Looks very well; states he feels definitely better and that during the past two weeks has been able to eat with apparent appetite, although he still insists on cutting down volume.

Examination Lungs: Entirely clear.

Heart: As before, apical impulse is in the anterior axillary line. The first sound at apex is of relatively good tone—A_2 is greater than P_2.

Abdomen: Soft—no masses.

X-ray Examination of Chest: Lung fields clear; cardiac measurements show no change over previous examinations; broad diameter 13.5.

Gall Bladder Series Done: Show good functional response; the double-dose oral method employing piradax produced excellent visualization of gall bladder.

X-ray Examination of gastro-intestinal tract shows no abnormalities.

Blood Picture: Red cells 4,200,000—white cells 7,400. Dis-

tribution of white cells not remarkable. Sedimentation
6 m.m.
Urine Concentration: 1.006 to 1.028.
Consultation conducted by Doctors Harper, Duncan,
Dickens, Behrens, and Bruenn.

Nevertheless, it was during the South Carolina stay,
when bronchitis was the President's one and only
trouble apart from fatigue, that the country filled with
every variety of wild and reckless lie about his physical condition. While satisfied with the accuracy of
the checks, I decided to leave no room for doubt, so
in the latter part of May I called in Dr. Paullin again,
and also Dr. Frank Lahey, head of the Lahey Clinic
in Boston. The President insisted that there was no
need for another going-over, and the examination bore
him out. Dr. Paullin and Dr. Lahey found that he had
recovered from the infection in his sinuses and chest,
and was "well and active," but the two did recommend
avoidance of overwork. What they urged was a rest
period after luncheon and free evenings, certainly after
nine o'clock, so that he could relax.

Dr. Paullin, in particular, made quite an impression
with one of his graphic comparisons. "Let's assume,"
he said, "that you're setting out on a fifty-thousand-
mile trip in a brand new machine. Good tires and the
engine hitting on every cylinder. After going forty
thousand miles, however, and with ten thousand miles
still ahead, you find definite signs of wear and tear.
There is a knock in the engine every now and then,

and while the body is pretty good, the tires are not in the best of shape.

"Mr. President, the engine and the tires are your heart and your arteries. I have used this story many times on men in high executive jobs, and here is the lesson to be learned: If you want to finish the journey, traveling the last ten thousand miles without mishap, you can't keep up any seventy-miles-an-hour clip. You've got to slow down to a speed that will not blow out the tires and wreck the engine. In plain words, you *must live within your reserve*."

The President laughed, although a bit ruefully. "Well, I'll agree to quit burning up the road," he promised. "Maybe not as slow as thirty miles an hour, but much less than seventy anyway." Taking immediate advantage of this concession, I sat down with him and worked out this daily routine:

8:30 to 9:00 A.M.—Breakfast in quarters
11:00 to 1:00 P.M.—Office—2 hours
1:00 P.M. to 2:00 P.M.—Luncheon in quarters
       No business guests
2:00 P.M. to 3:00 P.M.—Rest lying down
3:00 P.M. to 5:00 P.M.—Office—2 hours
45 minutes massage and ultraviolet light
    Rest before dinner—lying down
7:30 P.M. to 8:00 P.M.—Dinner in quarters
       No night work
       Sleep—10 hours
       Diet—Smooth—2,600 calories
       High vitamin additions

For a while he kept faithfully to this routine. Only in the matter of regaining weight was he recalcitrant, and a talk with the White House cook convinced me that he was cutting down on his diet deliberately. He gave the explanation that a lower poundage made walking easier, but I knew that the real reason was pride in his flat stomach.

What with the war load and domestic problems, the President also began to abandon his regimen, cutting out rest periods and working at night. More and more it became the habit to have luncheon served at his desk; and instead of inviting a few close friends in for dinner, as I had urged, he pored over papers as he ate. Harry Hopkins was a house guest, but while he assured me that he tried his best to keep the evenings "light," I never failed to find them with maps, reports, and memoranda, both tired and worn. Aside from the drudgery, I did not like the loneliness of it.

Anna Roosevelt Boettiger and the children were in Seattle, and the four boys were scattered over the various fighting fronts, leaving the President with a cold fear in his heart. Mrs. Roosevelt, caught in a web of official duties, was necessarily away much of the time. No one will ever know how much of his load she helped to carry, and how greatly she served him by tireless journeys that took her away from her husband, home, and children. During the war years with global questions demanding the President's time and attention to the exclusion of all else, Mrs. Roosevelt increasingly became his liaison with the domestic situation, invaluable by reason of her reports and interpretations.

My worry about the President's loneliness, fortunately enough, was not of long duration. With her soldier husband off on duty in the Mediterranean, Anna Boettiger closed her home in Seattle and came on to Washington. Always a gay and delightful companion, she had developed a very real executive ability through her newspaper experience, and she took hold of things with a firm hand. Not only did she succeed in persuading her father to build up his weight, but the after-luncheon siestas again became an order of the day. More than this, Anna guarded against night work, going through the papers that he brought over from the executive office and quietly weeding out all that could be handled by the secretariat. The presence of his beloved daughter bucked up the President no end, and under her watchful eye and constant care he began to look something like his old self.

A helpful improvement, for he was soon faced with another of those tremendous decisions from which his life permitted no escape. Would he stand for a fourth term?

CHAPTER XV

THE 1944 CAMPAIGN

Unlike 1940, when party leaders were fearful of the third-term tradition, 1944 saw them a unit in insisting that the President declare his willingness to accept renomination. After three terms Franklin Roosevelt dominated the national scene so completely that there was not another candidate in sight that held the least promise of success. His refusal to run again meant that the Republicans would win by default, and with this as a certainty the politicians exerted pressure instantly and powerfully.

Again I say that partisanship had no place in the President's mind, and again I insist that I am not guessing. During the weeks in which he delayed his decision, I talked with him and with members of the family, and out of these conversations came the firm and unchanging conviction that personal considerations were divorced from his thought. And again I ask, where was there any point in gulling me?

With the war at its most critical juncture and with victory in sight but still to be won, would he be justi-

191

fied in walking off the job? America's vast war machine had been built under his eyes and direction, and he knew every bolt and cog. Could untried hands take over without delay or hurt? During the long months intimate understandings had been built up with other Allied leaders, making for co-operative effort. Would they stand the strain and confusions of a change in administration?

What to do with Germany, when defeated, was also the President's deep concern. He had never forgotten the disastrous results of letting the Reich retain its potentialities as a military power after the First World War, and the equally disastrous failure to make the German people realize the fact of defeat. Not in any spirit of hate or revenge, but as a peace measure, he believed that Prussianism and militarism must be destroyed, root and branch, and the Germans themselves made to understand that their barbarities, either committed or condoned, were not to be viewed as regrettable errors but as crimes against the decencies of civilization. Would another, succeeding him, hold to the same belief?

Nearer than all else to his heart of hearts, however, was the United Nations, the great new world order that he hoped to bring into being on the day when the Axis Powers were crushed and suppliant. Though he was a devoted supporter of the League of Nations, not even its failure to fulfill high hopes had dimmed his faith in some form of international concert as the one means of preventing world wars and assuring world peace.

From the moment of Poland's invasion his mind had concerned itself with plans for such a concert, and the Atlantic Charter was in the nature of an opening gun. With America's entrance into the war, he had discussed the possibilities with Mr. Churchill, gaining his agreement, and Marshal Stalin had also approved in principle. Even so, it was still only a superstructure that waited for foundations. Victory, to him, was not merely the defeat of Germany and her willing and unwilling associates in ruthless totalitarianism, but the opportunity to establish an organization of peace that would usher in the reign of law and end forever the rule of might. Because he stood as the foremost protagonist of the United Nations, the builder of the ground plan, he believed devoutly yet humbly that his continuance in office might well mean the difference between success and failure.

As in 1940, a determining factor was his physical condition. Could he stand up under the strain of four more years? And again an affirmative answer was returned by consultants, for every possible checkup proved him organically sound. Although I have since been accused of making false and misleading reports on the President's health, my statements to the press simply reported the findings of specialists. Conjecture as to what *might* happen would have been grossly improper, nor was speculation the business of the physicians who conducted the examinations.

In private talk with the President, however, I could and did go beyond the checkups, frankly stating my fears. There was his age to be considered and twelve years of grueling strain such as no other chief executive had ever been called on to bear. With proper care and strict adherence to rules, I gave it as my best judgment that his chances of winning through to 1948 were *good*.

On the other hand, not even his incredible vitality and driving will could be expected to stand up against a continued disregard to every health rule. Unless he slowed down, I would not be answerable for the consequences. Hammering home my old warnings against the poisons of fatigue, I insisted on postluncheon naps and quiet evenings without night work. The President nodded agreement but put on his Dutch look when I brought up the question of his weight. Over and over, as I pressed the necessity of more poundage, he returned the answer that he felt fine.

"Well," I said at last, "you may feel fine, but you don't look it. Your neck is scrawny, and your face is gullied by a lot of lines that have added ten years to your age. And while we're on the subject," I added, "for heaven's sake, get some new clothes. That old shirt is sizes too large, and the coat hangs on your shoulders like a bag."

The President threw back his head and laughed,

but gave no promise, nor did he ever call in a tailor
or haberdasher. Generous in many ways, he was as
tight as Dick's hatband when it came to clothes. I
doubt if he ever threw a suit away, for as late as 1940
he was still wearing things I had seen on him in 1933.
His faithfulness to his old hats was demonstrated by
the appearance of the same ones in every campaign.
And the baggy coat and ill-fitting shirts, much too
large for his shrunken neck, did as much as anything
else to give an effect of illness and physical deterioration.

With the President all set to go, the selection of a
vice-presidential candidate became the concern of the
party leaders. It was a jumbled-up business from start
to finish, and to this day I am confused as to just what
happened. The beginning, I think, was a report by
Mr. Flynn, chairman of the Democratic National Committee, to the effect that the organization was opposed
to the renomination of Henry Wallace. Looking at the
situation from a purely political angle, Democratic
wheel horses felt that Mr. Wallace could not bring
any strength to the ticket, as his following was committed to the President anyway; while it was more than
probable that his reputation for a fairly extreme brand
of radicalism would alienate the party's right wing.

Accepting their judgment, despite his fondness for
Mr. Wallace, the President advanced the name of
Justice Douglas; and, until the final balloting took
place, I was under the impression that he would be

the nominee. As I gathered from other sources at a later date, party leaders turned thumbs down on the Justice, arguing that he was not well enough known, and also that the people might not like the idea of raiding the Supreme Court for a candidate.

The names of Mr. Byrnes and Senator Barkley were rejected, according to the story given me, on the ground that the choice of a Southerner might chill the enthusiasm of Negro voters. The selection of Senator Truman, therefore, was reached by a process of elimination. He was from a pivotal state, had made a good record as chairman of the so-called Truman Committee, and while a valiant New Dealer, had never carried his liberalism to a point where the conservatives viewed him with alarm.

I find it difficult to credit that the understanding had any such exactness. If so, I do not believe that the President would have permitted Justice Byrnes and Senator Barkley to go ahead with their candidacies. Certainly he said nothing to me, or to any others of the White House circle, that indicated an explicit agreement on Senator Truman as the nominee. I think it much more probable that after consenting to the elimination of Mr. Wallace, the President simply named the Senator as one who would be acceptable to him as a running mate.

The President's journey to the Pacific on the very eve of the convention in Chicago was attacked as a political maneuver, shrewdly designed to focus attention on him as the commander in chief rather than as a presidential candidate. Nothing was further from the truth. The war in Europe was going well; for our beachhead in Normandy was fully secured; General de Gaulle's visit to the White House had given promise of better co-operation with the Free French, and the Germans were retreating in Italy.

Attention, therefore, could be safely turned to the Pacific where the capture of Saipan, Tinian, and Guam seemed to be imminent. In view of these developments, both Admiral King and General Marshall urged the importance of an immediate conference with General MacArthur and Admiral Nimitz, and since these key figures could not leave their stations, the President went to them. Plans were arranged almost overnight, and as a result his acceptance speech was broadcast from our train at the Marine base in San Diego. Such was the need for haste that we boarded a cruiser the very next morning and set off for Pearl Harbor.

Not once on the voyage did the President mention the campaign or refer in any way to the coming election. His one thought was how to defeat Japan in the shortest possible time and with the least possible loss. The secret of the atomic bomb was locked in his breast, but there was an evening when he did drop a hint about the development of a weapon so terrible that its use would shock the world. I knew something about this work as I was called upon to furnish medical personnel for certain features of the project in which the Navy had a part. He admitted that the prospect appalled him, but if and when the weapon was perfected and employed, there was the justification that it would hasten the war's end and save a million American lives.

The President also commented with deep bitterness on the inhumanities of the Japanese. Reports of the death march from Bataan had shocked him to the depths, arousing an implacable resentment, and he was equally moved by the stories that came from the prison camps in China, Japan, and the Philippines. To crush the Japanese—to destroy Japan forever as a military power—had become an obsession that shut everything else out of his mind.

The three days of conference in Hawaii, beginning on July 26, stand and still stand as convincing answer to the charge that the President was a sick man. Of all the military, air, and naval leaders who sat with him, planning the final drive to crush Japan, there was not one who failed to comment on the vigor of his mind and the clarity of his thought. The delicate problems of area commands were solved amicably, and equally full agreement was reached on future operations.

The widespread report that the President did not like Douglas MacArthur had no base in truth. He may have smiled now and then at some of the General's purple communiqués, but always there was appreciation of him as a military genius who had worked miracles in the face of heartbreaking odds. Never at any time did I hear him speak of MacArthur except in sincere admiration, and it was out of his feeling that the General was too valuable to be endangered that he had ordered him to leave the Philippines before the capture of Bataan.

Admiral Nimitz had the same high place in his regard, both as a great human being and a brilliant officer. It both amused and irritated the President when speculation arose as to why he had not set up a supreme commander for the whole Pacific as was done in Europe. "Our typewriter strategists," he once remarked, "ought to take a primary course in oceanography. None of them seems to realize that the Pacific covers 66,634,000 square miles."

Every day in Hawaii was crowded, and yet the President found the time and strength to visit every war installation from the great naval base at Pearl Harbor to isolated posts on the mountaintops, regardless of weather. Not only that, but he went into the jungle country at Kahana Bay where our men were being taught the sort of fighting that they would have to encounter in Pacific islands. Sniping, infiltration, assaults on log pillboxes, hip-shooting, crossing makeshift bridges, and hand-to-hand struggles in villages.

I offered no objection to these activities, knowing his eager interest, but I did try to get him to forego the inspection of troops. Standing any length of time put a heavy strain on his muscles, invariably bringing

199

on a backache; but he was always unfailingly punctilious where soldiers and sailors were concerned. In 1934 while inspecting troops he stood an hour and a half taking salutes and smiling at the boys as they marched by. So in 1944 when he reviewed the Seventh Division we prevailed upon him to stay seated in his automobile on the reviewing platform.

In accordance with his unfailing habit, he also visited every hospital on the islands, leaving his car and wheeling through the wards. At Schofield Barracks there were many Japanese-Americans wounded in Italy; in Honolulu most of the patients were from Saipan, and in the five-thousand-bed naval hospital on top of Aiea Heights there were men from the battles of Guam and Saipan. Aside from stopping at bedsides, at every place he made a short but stirring, encouraging speech to the shattered men; and I still get a lump in my throat when I remember the way they tried to lift their heads and cheer.

Not the least impressive moment of the whole Hawaiian stay was when the President rode through long lines of Japanese-American soldiers drawn up in single file. There was some effort to dissuade him out of the fear that there might be a fanatic in the ranks who would leap at the chance to shoot the President at point-blank range. "Nonsense!" he exclaimed. "I would never forgive myself if I shamed them by an open showing of their President's distrust."

One of the decisions of the conference involved the

assault on Iwo Jima, that pin-point island some two hundred miles off the coast of Japan. When the news came that it had cost us 22,763 casualties, the whole country was shocked; and the President himself knew deep distress. Before his death, thank God, he had the relief of knowing that the sacrifice of all those lives had not been in vain. Iwo Jima became a "spot of heaven" to our flyers, for it was a landing field that saved countless lives besides contributing immeasurably to the shortening of the war. When I was on the island in July 1945, I saw eighty-three B-29 bombers land in a single night, not one of which could have made it back to the Marianas after bombing Japan.

From Pearl Harbor the President went to the Aleutians, and here again is testimony as to his fitness. At Adak even a storm did not keep him under cover and after a morning of inspection, he lunched in a Quonset-hut mess hall flanked by servicemen. As young as the youngest there, he soon had all of them talking, and I can still remember the way he threw back his head and laughed after one exchange—a redheaded Marine from Arkansas, asked what he missed the most, promptly shot back, "Our girls."

All through our stay in the Aleutians the weather was abominable, with storms, incessant rain, and high seas. Our departure from Adak was delayed a full day, and on reaching Kodiak Island, a heavy fog held us up for six hours at the harbor entrance. Always a good sailor, the President took it in his stride, and on the way to Auke Bay even braved an icy downpour to try some fishing from the side of the ship. A stop at Bremerton, where he was scheduled for a speech, gave me the worst scare of the trip. To my consternation it had been arranged for him to speak from the forecastle deck of a destroyer; and, by the time I had discovered it, there was no time to change. A stiff wind was blowing, and there was quite a slant to the deck, two things that called for bracing on his part, and as a result he finished up with considerable pain. Purely muscular, as it turned out; and when we got back to Washington on August 17, after journeying 13,912 miles, he was in better shape than when we left.

All through the spring and early summer, Mr. Churchill had been importuning the President for another meeting of the Big Three. His first proposal was for an Easter session in Bermuda, and later on he urged London. Shortly after the President's return from the Pacific, the Prime Minister renewed his request, suggesting Scotland as a rendezvous. This was agreeable to the President, but Marshal Stalin refused on the ground that he could not take time away from the campaign. Mr. Churchill then asked a September conference with F.D.R. in Quebec, jovially arguing that Canada was eminently superior to Washington as a summer resort.

All arrangements were made, and our start was from Hyde Park, where the President went for the week end. Admiral Leahy, Admiral Wilson Brown, Steve

Early, General Watson, and I joined him there on Sunday morning, September 10. After one of his "country breakfasts," F.D.R. took us over the grounds and at every foot of the way pointed out improvements he had planned. "Now," he said, and there was sadness in his tone, "who knows when I will ever get to them."

At Quebec, aside from operations in Europe, Mr. Churchill's principal concern was to have Great Britain given opportunity for a more prominent part in the war against Japan. He pressed hard for the employment of the British fleet and was most reluctant to recognize that months of training would be required before His Majesty's ships were able to operate effectively in the Pacific.

What brought him around was an afternoon in the map room that we had set up in the Citadel. Before leaving Washington the President had ordered the preparation of charts, organization tables, and graphs that would show the tremendous size of our naval force in the western Pacific and the enormity of the logistics problem. After studying the display himself and listening to the experts, Mr. Churchill somewhat ruefully admitted that the situation seemed to be too well in hand for any change.

It seemed to me, and this was not only my own opinion, that the President and the Prime Minister worked more amicably and smoothly together than at any previous time, as a result of better understandings and what had become a very real friendship. Just before leaving the Citadel for our train, Mr. Churchill requested me to come to his room, and asked for a confidential statement as to the President's physical condition, explaining that he had been alarmed by reports.

I gave him the results of our June checkup, proving that there was nothing organically wrong, but not hesitating to stress the President's age and the fact that for twelve years he had been under constant strain. If, I said, he does not overdo, there is every reason to believe that he can win through. "With all my heart I hope so," and the Prime Minister's voice rang with deep feeling. "We cannot have anything happen to this man. His usefulness to the world is paramount during these troubled times."

From the close of the Quebec conference up to election day, the President's physical examinations were frequent, and all of them, throughout the entire time, showed few variations. Since it is now a fixed habit of certain columnists to assert that Franklin Roosevelt was a dying man in 1944 and that his medical advisers were well aware of it, I submit this typical checkup, covering the period from September 20 to November 1:

Temperature—98.6—no elevations; general appearance—color good; present weight—172.

Lungs clear; heart—no cardiac symptoms at any time—sounds are good in character; pulse rate ranges 68 to 74.

Blood pressure of labile type; systolic ranging from 165 to 180; diastolic from 88 to 100; electrocardiogram shows no changes from that of May examination; patient more relaxed and at ease; it is noted that only small annoyances cause any rise in systolic pressure.

Kidney function—normal; liver function—normal; blood picture—shows no anemia or any abnormality; blood chemistry—all levels in normal limits—sedimentation rate in normal range.

Conclusion—general condition satisfactory; rest routine must be continued.

Cardiovascular system shows moderate arteriosclerosis—retinal vessels appear normal—dilution—concentration tests—urine—1.004-1.028. Completely satisfactory.

Patient underweight. No changes in diet recommended except more vitamins.

Consultants—Drs. Harper, Duncan, Behrens, Dickens, and Bruenn.

I have not translated the medical phraseology into layman's language, not wishing to be accused of paraphrasing; but any doctor going over it will bear out my statement, made to the press, that the President was in "good condition for a man of his age." Tired, of course, and underweight, but organically sound.

In his speech of acceptance the President had made this explicit announcement of purpose: "I shall not campaign in the usual sense for the office. In these days of tragic sorrow I do not consider it fitting. Besides, in these days of global warfare, I shall not be able to find the time." This was in accordance with my urgent request. While admitting that he *could* travel and make speeches, I pointed out the danger of overexertion, and the necessity of guarding his reserves. He agreed to confine himself to a few radio addresses, and I am confident that he would have kept to this pledge but for the tactics of the opposition. As the President saw it, the Republican nominee was back in his old role of prosecutor, and not any too careful about his methods of securing a conviction. All of us could see F.D.R.'s growing resentment and knew that an explosion was due.

Another compelling reason for a change in decision was the revival of the "rumor factories." From the opening of the campaign until its close, not a day passed without the circulation of some new and alarming rumor about the physical and mental condition of the President. All of the whispers charged growing incapacity and even actual collapse; but aside from this, there was no agreement. At one and the same time he was reported to be suffering from a coronary thrombosis, a brain hemorrhage, a nervous breakdown, an aneurysm in the aorta, and a cancerous prostate. Now he was supposed to be in a Miami sanitarium under the observation of specialists, and now in a Chicago hospital with eminent surgeons gathered for an operation. For weeks on end the White House was flooded with anxious inquiries.

Deeply angered by these malignant falsehoods, the President waved my objections aside and scheduled

206

speeches in Washington, New York, Boston, and Chicago. The best I could get from him was a promise to sit while speaking. This, by the way, was no new argument but one that had been going on since 1933. The steel braces, despite skillful manufacture and careful adjustment, were painful when Mr. Roosevelt kept on his feet for any length of time, and I had never seen the sense of having him take punishment.

Standing did not exercise the muscles of the legs, as did swimming, but merely subjected them to ache and strain. Why expect a man of sixty-three, just getting over the flu and still troubled with bronchitis, to run three miles at top speed? This, I explained, was the exact amount of physical effort that would be required if the President stood in his steel braces for forty-five minutes.

The Washington dinner passed off well, but New York greeted our arrival with a rainstorm that never once let up. Nothing could dissuade the President from riding through the streets in an open car, but he did consent to let himself be bundled up, putting a heavy sweater on inside his Navy boat cloak and wrapping blankets around his legs. At Ebbets Field, however, he threw off his coverings and got on the stand to make a short talk in behalf of Senator Wagner, an old and dear friend. My protests went unheeded; but afterward, by way of amends, he let us hustle him to a near-by Coast Guard station, where there was a brisk rubdown and a change of clothes from the skin out.

Except for weather, the Boston engagement held even more possibilities of strain than New York. We left Washington at night and stopped at Bridgeport early on the following morning for a talk from the back platform of the train. At Hartford the President made a speech in the open, and in response to the clamor of gathered thousands, gave another from the back platform at Springfield, Massachusetts. He stood in his braces for all of them. In spite of the hard day, he was at his best in Boston's Fenway Park that night.

The Chicago speech drew a crowd that filled every seat in enormous Soldiers' Field; and here again his voice had the old ring and authority. Unfortunately, a cold wind blew in from the lake, and the President confessed to having been chilled from start to finish. This worried me, but one of George Fox's rubs brought him to a glow, and he reached Washington in high spirits and without so much as a sniffle.

CHAPTER XVI

YALTA

QUITE FRANKLY, I HAD DREADED THE CAMPAIGN; BUT the manner in which the President came through it made me doubt my accuracy as a diagnostician. Being more than ten pounds underweight had not dulled the edge of his energy, and even his sinuses had acted handsomely. He was tired, of course, and confessed it, but gaily confident that a week or so in Warm Springs would work the usual miracle. Unhappily, he ran into cold, rainy weather, and the expected benefits did not materialize.

Back at the White House, pressure increased instead of lightening, for along with a host of domestic problems, there was a disturbing swing of things in Europe and Asia. While the Russian offensive was making rapid progress geographically, it had been delayed so long that a large part of the press in Great Britain and the United States were beginning to doubt Stalin's intention to destroy Germany's military power. There were even hints at a separate peace. The Chinese situation continued to be discouraging because of the re-

209

fusal of the Communists to co-operate with Chiang Kai-shek, and a suspicion grew that this attitude proceeded from Russian influence.

The question of Poland and the Baltic states agitated public opinion in the United States, and both in Congress and out bitter complaints were being made against what appeared to be unilateral action on the part of Russia with respect to the whole of eastern Europe. Even more importantly, there was as yet no agreement among the Big Three as to the organization of the United Nations. As Mr. Churchill phrased it, Marshal Stalin continued to be a "riddle wrapped in an enigma."

Thus my worst worry was not in the campaign but between election day and the inauguration. This period, in fact, was the most distressing in the whole of my experience as White House physician. The President did not seem able to rid himself of a sense of terrible urgency, and even Anna Boettiger could not keep him from working through the entire day and well into the night. Physical and mental strain, plus loss of appetite, reduced his weight to 170 pounds, deepening the lines already in his face and adding new ones. Any reminder of the promise to live within his reserves brought the old answer that there was a job to be done.

At that, the checkups were not alarming: "Color fair; lies flat without dyspnea (difficulty in breathing); eye grounds show no retinal sclerosis; lungs clear;

heart-sounds clear and of good quality; liver and kidneys functioning normally; no gastrointestinal symptoms; blood pressure ranges from 170/88 to 188/100; appears very tired." Nevertheless, the heart reserve had to be watched, and Dr. Bruenn's care was unremitting. With his usual extraordinary capacity to rise to the occasion, however, the President delivered his inaugural address with every appearance of vigor, and only the White House circle knew his weariness.

So it was that I welcomed his announcement that another conference of the Big Three was going to be held. A sea voyage, at least, would get him away from his desk and give him a week of rest. The President's original suggestion, made early in January, was for a meeting in the Mediterranean area, but Marshal Stalin refused to leave the security provided by his soldiers and secret police, and insisted that some Russian city had to be chosen. Odessa was first mentioned, but I vetoed it as unsanitary and rejected several other places for the same reason. F.D.R. finally remembered that the Crimea had been a favorite summer and winter resort of the czars, and Ambassador Harriman was asked to investigate its possibilities. When he reported that several palaces were in good condition, the President decided on Yalta, and Marshal Stalin hastened to approve.

The party that left Washington on January 22 was larger than usual, consisting of the President, Anna Roosevelt Boettiger, Admiral Leahy, War Mobilizer

James F. Byrnes, Edward Flynn, General Watson, Steve Early, Admiral Wilson Brown, and myself. Going by train to Norfolk, we boarded the U.S.S. *Quincy*, and as a German submarine was reported off the coast, the cruiser *Savannah* escorted us in addition to our usual convoy of three destroyers.

Several days before reaching Malta, where we were to change from ship to plane, disconcerting messages began to come in from Mr. Churchill. Ten years of patient research, he claimed, could not have found a worse place than Yalta. It was "good only for typhus and deadly lice," and as if that were not bad enough, the approaching roads were "frightening and at times impassable." The President, however, laughed off these gloomy predictions as proceeding from the Prime Minister's irritation at Stalin's refusal to meet in the Mediterranean area.

At Malta we switched from the *Quincy* to a C-54 for the 1,700-mile flight to the Crimea. On both the Casablanca and Teheran trips, the President's plane had been equipped with ramps, but I had never liked them; and, as a result of my insistence, our ship was now fitted up with an elevator which lowered to the ground level to facilitate embarking and disembarking. Some improvements had also been made in sleeping arrangements, so that a more restful night was assured.

We were met at Malta by Secretary of State Stettinius and his corps of assistants, and also by the joint Chiefs of Staff and their planning sections. Getting away from the island, therefore, was quite a transport problem, for some seven hundred people were involved. Starting around ten o'clock that night, huge planes took off at ten-minute intervals. Air-sea rescue ships were stationed in the Aegean and Black Seas, and the President's plane was escorted by six fighters.

It was the first real acquaintance with the new Secretary of State for most of us, and there was the fact that Mr. Stettinius labored under the disadvantage of following a man like Cordell Hull. Before our return to the United States, however, he had earned the liking and respect of the entire American delegation. Never was anything more cruelly unfair than the sneer that he was selected to succeed Mr. Hull because the President intended to be his own Secretary of State. Since Stettinius was a new man, taking over the high office from one who had held it for twelve years, there was much that the President had to handle himself, but as the Secretary grew in experience, he was increasingly a strong right hand.

Saki, our landing field, was ninety miles from Yalta, but Mr. Molotov was on hand to greet us, supported by crack troops and a fine military band. Mr. Churchill's plane followed us in, and after the speeches and music we loaded into cars and jolted off over a road that lived up to the Prime Minister's dark description. A Sherman tank would have found it tough going, and six long hours passed before we drew up in front of the Livadia palace, our home for the next eight days.

Formerly the summer residence of the czars, and built on a terrace high above the Black Sea, the palace sprawled far and wide in every direction, each room large enough for a skating rink. The President's suite, once sacred to the use of Czar Nicholas, consisted of a reception room, a sitting room, a bedroom formerly the billiard room, and a conference chamber that had served as a ballroom–banquet hall in the time of the czars. All of the ceilings were twenty-five feet high and supported by massive marble columns. Magnificent but anything but homey.

In view of the fact that the Germans had occupied all of the buildings in Yalta until a recent date, and suspecting that they had not been very particular about upkeep, I had taken precautions well in advance. Through our fleet surgeon in the Mediterranean, I had arranged for the organization of a competent team of doctors and hospital corpsmen who knew how to clean up infected areas. Shortly before our arrival, the *Catoctin* steamed through the Dardanelles into the Black Sea, then on to Sevastopol, carrying all the necessities needed for the subsistence of the American delegation while in Yalta.

Admiral Olson, the officer in command, reported to me that he threw up both hands at first sight of the palace, doubting that it could ever be made livable. The plumbing, although recently installed, functioned poorly; but worst of all was the dirt and abounding animal and insect life. Russian laborers were put to work at once, and after the grime of years had been removed, a 10-per-cent solution of D.D.T. in kerosene was brought into play.

Every bed, piece of bedding, rug, and hanging in the palace was given at least three thorough sprayings, and then dusted with D.D.T. talcum-powder mixture. Daily inspections were made the rule, and at sight of an insect of any sort an alarm was sounded. Our British friends soon called for help, but while we also offered assistance to the Russians, they refused, although thanking us kindly.

Along with sanitation the Russian dinners were also a prime worry, for the courses ran in this order: caviar and vodka, smoked fish, broiled fish, soup, lamb or mutton, salad, preserved fruits, pies and cakes, and wines that the waiters never stopped pouring. Rich foods, fortunately, had never appealed to the President; and it did not need my warnings to make him eat sparingly of the simpler dishes and do no more than wet his lips in response to the innumerable toasts. At Mr. Churchill's birthday party the gathering drank his health thirty-four times by actual count.

Judged by Russian standards, Marshal Stalin would, I imagine, be regarded as fairly temperate, but from the American viewpoint he was a lusty trencherman and equally good at "bottoms up." Whether it was the vodka and champagne or a growing affection I am not able to say, but toward the last of the dinners he left his seat quite regularly to pat the President on the back.

As he did not extend this genial massage of the shoulder blades to the Prime Minister, I like to believe that it was affection.

Whatever quarrel our party might have had with the sanitation and the interminable dinners, we certainly had no fault to find with the Marshal's security precautions. They were even more elaborate than those at Teheran. Armed guards and secret police were under our feet at every step, and the Yalta streets and approaches were heavily patrolled—mostly by young girls, not more than fifteen, carrying bayoneted rifles. The completeness of Russia's mobilization made our own look partial, for not only were there almost as many women as men in the factories and fields, but I saw them in the ranks with full soldier's equipment.

The conferences began at once and continued through the week almost without a break. As a result of malicious and persistent propaganda, it has come to be accepted as a fact that the President was not himself at Yalta, either physically or mentally, and functioned merely as a rubber stamp for Marshal Stalin, weakly yielding to his demands at every point.

I said then, and I say now, that these charges were every whit as false and baseless as the whisper about his breakdown in Teheran. It is true that the President was worn out when he left Washington, not because of the campaign but entirely as a result of the press of affairs between the election and his inauguration. The days at sea, however, had their usual tonic effect, and he reached Yalta in fine fettle. The sessions were long and exhausting, and there were evenings when he confessed to being "pretty well fagged," but never once was there a loss of vigor and clarity.

Much of the talk, in my opinion, was occasioned by newspaper pictures. In earlier years photographers had been uniformly kind and thoughtful, never snapping him in an awkward position, such as adjusting his braces or transferring to a wheel chair. Toward the last, however, they shot him from every angle and seemed to prefer the pictures that caught him with his mouth open or stooped forward. Many photographs taken at Yalta were excellent, showing him alive and alert; but for the most part the papers printed flashlights that gave the President a ghastly pallor and accentuated the thinness of his face.

Like everybody else outside of the Big Three, I knew nothing of the agreements made behind closed doors, but I did know what the President had in mind when he went to the Crimean conference. As was his habit, the President talked frankly to a few of us, for it was a favorite method of crystallizing and clarifying his own thoughts.

Of first importance was the desire to bring Russia into the war with Japan. At the time there was no hint of Japan's collapse, and the President's military advisers estimated that our casualties might reach the staggering total of one million if the struggle dragged on.

Russian aid meant an earlier victory and the saving of American lives.

Secondly, the President believed that a strong, united China was not only essential to the Allied war effort, but to the peace that would follow victory. What he wanted, therefore, was a promise from Marshal Stalin that he would withdraw support from the Communists and back the Central Government of Chiang Kai-shek; also full recognition of Manchuria as a Chinese possession.

Thirdly, the President wanted a settlement of the Polish question that would recognize the right of that unhappy country to full sovereignty. Not only was there the fact of Poland's heroic resistance—even when five million of her people were dead of torture or starvation, the Germans could not find a Quisling—but Polish armies were battling side by side with the Allies on every front. There were few things about which the President felt more deeply, and while conscious that compromises might have to be made, he stood unchangeably for the reconstitution of Poland as a sovereign and independent state.

The fourth point for which he meant to fight was Russia's immediate, open, and sincere adherence to the United Nations. Stalin had given his promise at the Teheran conference but since then he had engaged in many unilateral actions and made no secret of his preference for the continued rule of the Big Three. Persistence in this attitude meant that the United

Nations would either fall to pieces or else get off to a slow and painfully limping start.

The President's views on Communism, expressed as we voyaged to Teheran, had undergone some fundamental changes. While still convinced that Marxism could not endure as a system of government, he now recognized the ideology as a disruptive force. Moscow's agents, if given the order, could and would bring about chaos in conquered countries and make for profound disturbance elsewhere. Already Tito had established an insolent dictatorship in Yugoslavia; and France, under Russian pressure, had been compelled to accept the return of Thorez, a fugitive in Moscow after being sentenced to death by a French court for his treasons. Unless Stalin could be induced to join wholeheartedly with the Allies, keeping his ideology for home consumption, the very worst was to be feared.

How much would have to be given as a price for Stalin's agreement on all four points and the promise of postwar co-operation? The President did not know, but he was prepared to bid high. Nor was he in any doubt as to the element of gamble involved. If Stalin did sign on the dotted line, where was the guarantee that he would continue to honor his signature? What minimized this risk was the President's conviction that Russia, in spite of boasts, stood in desperate need of the peace that would give time and opportunity for the work of reconstruction, the development of resources, and the attainment of a decent standard of living.

219

Six formal sessions of the Crimea conference were held, all in the grand ballroom of the Livadia. Also, in addition to the many luncheons and dinners, the Marshal came frequently to the President's sitting room for private and informal talks. I may be mistaken, of course, for the Russian face is not an open book by any means, but I believed then, and still believe, that Stalin had a very real liking and respect for F.D.R. I watched many of their meetings, and as the two came together, the Marshal's eyes would lose their hard, shrewd, "trading" look and take on warmth. If it was all an act, then he was a mighty good actor.

Every day just before dinner I had Lieutenant Commander George Fox give the President an alcohol rub and light massage, and each night I went in for a bedtime chat. On these occasions he would run over the high lights of the day, not so much for my information, I imagine, but more to fix them in his own mind. The first formal meeting was held on Sunday, and the initial sessions were discouraging. Stalin still rode a high horse and, to mix my metaphors a bit, made it quite plain that he thought himself in the driver's seat.

I was able, fortunately, to contribute some corroborative evidence in support of the President's belief that Russia was in bad shape and would welcome a period of peace at the war's end. I had become fairly friendly with some of the Russian officers, and one conversation in particular was most enlightening.

"Why," I asked them, "do you still keep your Iron

Curtain? What is your idea in refusing to let the Americans and the British get behind it? Don't you trust us?"

"The question of trust," they answered, "doesn't enter into it at all. It is simply that we don't want our people to see you or hear you. Russia, quite frankly, is about where your country was one hundred years ago. All the various Plans have done little to raise the standards of living. We have managed, however, to keep the people more or less contented by telling them that conditions are much worse in the outside world. If we let you and the British in, they might learn differently."

Whether it was Russia's plight, or whether other considerations changed Stalin's mind, the situation bettered toward the end of the week. On Friday evening, I found the President hitting on high, and it was with his old smile that he announced, "I've got everything I came for, and not at too high a price."

Russia, he said, would enter the war against Japan at an early date; and not only had Stalin agreed to full participation in the organization of the United Nations, but San Francisco was to be the host city for the first meeting. This last news delighted me particularly, for Steve Early and I, at a bull session a few nights before, had urged San Francisco as a natural in view of the growing emphasis on the war in the Pacific.

The Polish settlement, the President confessed, left a good deal to be desired. The Chinese understanding, however, was more than satisfactory. At an early date Russia would negotiate a treaty of friendship and alliance with Chiang Kai-shek. As a further evidence of Russian intent with respect to China's territorial integrity, Manchuria would be acknowledged as a Chinese possession. In addition, there was to be an announcement of absolute noninterference in China's internal affairs, and full recognition of the Communist issue as a purely domestic problem.

The rotten situation in Yugoslavia was also remedied by the agreement that Tito's dictatorship should give way to a new coalition government, and that all of Tito's acts would be subject to review by a new parliament.

On Sunday the report of the Crimea conference, signed by the President, the Prime Minister, and Marshal Stalin, was duly issued, and bore out the President's statements in every detail. Faith in the principles of the Atlantic Charter was reaffirmed, and the right of all liberated peoples to sovereignty and self-government explicitly guaranteed.

The existing Polish Provisional Government, then purely Russian, was to be "reorganized on a broader democratic basis with the inclusion of democratic leaders from Poland itself and from Poles abroad." The new Polish Provisional Government of National Unity stood pledged to "the holding of free and unfettered elections as soon as possible on the basis of universal suffrage and secret ballot. In these elections all democratic and anti-Nazi parties shall have the right to take part and put forward candidates." Much the same formula was announced with respect to Yugoslavia.

The "earliest possible establishment with our allies of a general international organization to maintain peace and security" was no less a solemn pledge; and April 25, 1945, was the date set for the San Francisco meeting at which a charter would be prepared.

And now a word as to price. In return for her agreement to enter the war against Japan, Russia was promised the Kurile Islands, a stone's throw off the Russian coast, and the southern half of Sakhalin. A large reward, at first glance, but not when balanced against a million American lives.

For his engagement to enter wholeheartedly into the organization of the new world order, abandoning unilateral actions and "lone wolf" tactics, Russia was given two additional seats in the U.N. assembly. Not in the all-powerful Security Council, mind you, but in the *Assembly*. The alternative was to have the Soviet Union stay outside the family of nations, a continual source of disruption.

The Polish settlement, as the President admitted, was a bitter pill to swallow. He had never liked the so-called Curzon line, and felt that the handing over of east Poland to Russia was shabby treatment for a brave people. But Great Britain, Poland's original ally, sided with Russia in the matter of the Curzon line, and there was the added fact that Russian troops were advancing on Poland with the nearest Allied army far away. In plain, it was a case of like it or lump it, and the President chose to like it out of the hope that the promised coalition government, also the free elections that Stalin had pledged, would work a change in Russian policy.

The division of a conquered Germany into occupational zones was another pill, but here again the situation was much the same as with Poland. The Allied thrust against Germany was from the west, with Russians making the only advance on the east. Victory, therefore, would find the Russians in possession of the whole eastern half of Germany, and what was to be done about that?

Much has since been said and written about the secrecy that surrounded the price paid to Russia in return for her agreements, but not a word as to the reasons for this secrecy. Because of the fact that Russia was still at peace with Japan, how was it possible to give publicity to her promise to join forces with the Allies in the Pacific? The same consideration held back any mention of the Chinese understanding. As for the charge that President Roosevelt played a lone hand, keeping all of his associates in the dark, I do not believe that it will be sustained by former Secretary of State Stettinius or the heads of the armed forces.

I am no politician, and it may well be that devotion warps my judgment, but I have never been able to see where the Yalta agreements deserved to be attacked as fawning appeasement and shameful surrender. It is true that many have not been kept, and that others have been tortured out of their original intent by word twisting; but how does that invalidate the bargains themselves? And I think it worthy of note that there were no significant departures from good faith until the death of the President. Had he lived, I believe with all my heart that every Yalta pledge would have been kept; for those who gave them would not have dared to risk his excoriations.

On our return to the United States I made it my business to collect the editorial comment of the principal metropolitan dailies on the conference. Now that Yalta is being attacked as the appeasements of a sick man, it is interesting to go over them and institute a before-and-after comparison.

The New York *Times* said that the agreements "justify and surpass most of the hopes placed on this fateful meeting," and called the reaffirmation of the Atlantic Charter "the most important point." The New York *Herald Tribune* editorialized that "the Conference has produced another great proof of Allied unity, strength and power of decision." The Washington *Post*, anything but Rooseveltian, congratulated the President "on his part in this all-encompassing achievement." Only a few "bitter end" dailies refused to join in the chorus of praise. Maybe none of this proves anything, but I find it mighty pleasant reading.

CHAPTER XVII

THE THREE KINGS

THE CRIMEA CONFERENCE DID NOT END THE LIST OF presidential chores, for next on the schedule were meetings in Egypt with King Farouk; Haile Selassie, Emperor of Ethiopia; and Abdul-Aziz ibn Abdul-Rahman al-Faisal ibn-Saud, King of Saudi Arabia. Not an easy assignment after eight days of argument and persuasion, and the manner in which the President came through furnished further disproof of the charge that he was a failing man suffering from coronary thrombosis, cancer, kidney infection, premature senility, and everything else that occurred to the minds of malicious gossips.

It had been arranged for us to drive directly from Livadia to the airfield at Saki, but the President's generous thoughtfulness led to a change in plan. Once in the car, he insisted on going to Sevastopol that he might have a chance to thank the officers and crew of the *Catoctin* for their drudging labors as a sanitary squad. The eighty-mile journey took us over rough mountain roads, but the President's eager interest in the scene of the Light Brigade's historic charge left him no time for discomfort.

Starting out at six o'clock the next morning, we drove ninety miles to the airfield at Saki, where we boarded our plane shortly before noon and were back in Egypt, on the *Quincy*, anchored in the Great Bitter Lake, in the late afternoon. This flight was carried out in something around six hours' time and the average altitude was 8,000 feet; at one time, flying over the high mountains on the southern shores of Turkey, it was necessary to go up to around 11,000 feet. This caused no discomfort to the President, who had never shown any signs of anoxemia when flying at altitudes around 10,000 to 12,000 feet. Everybody rejoiced in the prospect of shower baths and real American food. Especially baths, for despite Livadia's grandeur, there were but two tubs. Of course, one was given over to the President, and the rest of us had been forced to depend on daily scrubs with a wet towel.

King Farouk was our first visitor, staying for luncheon. An amiable, unassuming gentleman, remarkable only for his perfect English and open admiration for F.D.R. The talk was chiefly concerned with two-way future trade relations, the King stressing the merits of his long-staple cotton. Haile Selassie came on board at four and never left until seven, for the President had long admired his courage. A grave, unsmiling little man standing only five feet three inches, he did not look very much like the Elect of God and the Conquering

Lion of the Tribe of Judah. Nevertheless, he bore himself with dignity and gave an impression of character and force. We had looked for a colorful show by the Ethiopians, but they were about as barbaric as a bunch of Rotarians. The Emperor himself wore a plain khaki uniform, but the Cabinet members were all modern and dapper in civilian attire. Not a lion's skin or spear in the lot.

The next day, however, left nothing to be desired in the way of color, for the arrival of ibn-Saud swung us out of the twentieth century into a distant and barbaric past. The U.S.S. *Murphy* had picked him up at Jidda, a Saudi Arabian port on the Red Sea; for it was the first time that the King had ever left his native soil, and the President wished to show appreciation of the compliment. When the *Murphy* steamed into view at the lower end of the lake, around ten o'clock, it looked more like an Oriental pavilion than an American man-of-war. The forecastle blazed with rare rugs, the royal guard gave an additional note of color, as did a picturesque huddle of slaves in the background. Ibn-Saud himself, magnificent in flowing robes and jewels, sat enthroned in a brocaded chair on the gun deck.

According to the official bulletin, his entourage numbered forty-eight people, and besides the royal family and Cabinet members, included an astrologer, a royal purse bearer, the chief server of ceremonial coffee, an official food taster, and a chaplain who sounded the call for prayer. As the *Murphy* drew near, we could plainly hear the bleat of sheep, for the King traveled with his own commissary.

Ibn-Saud came on board with his brother, his two sons, and several members of the Cabinet; and, as they went through the exchange of ceremonial salutations, I could see that the President was getting a great kick out of it. Another thrill was provided at luncheon when the royal taster gravely sampled every bit of food and drink before letting it reach the royal mouth. Ibn-Saud courteously explained it as an ancient custom, as was the large jug containing water from two holy wells.

As near as I could judge, the King was around seventy, and besides a perceptible lameness, had cataracts in both eyes. None of this, however, seemed to impair his vigor, for his arguments gave the President a bad hour. At the very outset of their formal conference, ibn-Saud protested continued Jewish immigration into Palestine and declared that the Arabs would "choose to die rather than yield their lands to the Jews."

When the President interrupted to ask what Saudi Arabia had to do with Palestine, His Majesty answered that he was the leader of the Wahhabis, guardians of the Holy Places of Mecca and Medina. As such, he considered himself the world's foremost Moslem, and an authoritative spokesman for the Arabs with respect to the Jewish problem.

The President, in reply, contented himself with the diplomatic assurance that Americans held the Arab people in friendship and high regard and expressed the hope that the Palestinian question would be worked out in amity and with justice to all. From subsequent discussions I am sure that at no time was anything said that could justify the King's later statement that the President had supported the Arab position.

Ibn-Saud then brought up the question of Syria and Lebanon and asked to be told the attitude of the United States in the event that France continued to press "intolerable demands." The President replied that the French Government had given him, in writing, a guarantee of the independence of Syria and Lebanon, and he had no doubt that this word would be honored.

It was plain to see that the President did not like these controversial subjects and made repeated attempts to switch the conversation. Mentioning the barrenness of the land as seen from the air, he plunged into a dissertation on what could be done to turn the arid land into an Eden.

"Never sell your oil," he urged. "Lease it on a royalty basis. With the money you can tap the hidden streams that lie under the soil of Arabia. Irrigation will make your valleys green again and cover your hill slopes with forests. And there is the development of water power that will give you light and heat and turn the wheels of industry." All this was followed by a glowing picture of America's reclamation projects, with rosy descriptions of Boulder Dam, the TVA, and the Grand Coulee.

The effort fell flatter than a Mexican tortilla; that night, in a bull session, the President ruefully admitted it. Old ibn-Saud listened without the bat of an eye or the twitch of a muscle and then took up right where he had left off. Arabia, it was true, needed many things, but where was the point in improvement as long as the Palestinian question remained unsettled? How could he be expected to engage in the development of his country's agriculture and public works if the resultant prosperity would be "inherited by the Jews"? And that was that!

With state matters finished, however, and out of the way, ibn-Saud returned to amiability and betrayed a lively interest in personal things—guns, planes, and particularly penicillin. I was summoned, together with the royal physician; and, on finding that they held the drug in almost superstitious esteem as a miracle worker, I presented them with 500,000 units out of the ship's store. Another exciting gift was made by the President. At first sight of one of F.D.R.'s wheel chairs, ibn-Saud's eyes bugged out, and when he made several pointed references to that "superb device for conserving energy," the President took the hint. As the King went over the side with his chair and his penicillin, not all of his oriental passivity could hide his delight. As for the royal physician, he fairly wiggled.

Poor Anna Boettiger! She had been an invaluable aid both on the journey to Yalta and all through the conferences, helping me to ride herd on the President and seeing to it that he obeyed orders with respect to rest and diet. With just as much enthusiasm as her father, she had looked forward to seeing ibn-Saud and his entourage, having all of his eager interest in everything new. On reaching the Great Bitter Lake, we learned that while the King had a decided fondness for women in the quiet of private life, the customs of his country barred them from public affairs. As a consequence, Anna spent the day in Cairo, sight-seeing and shopping.

Weighing anchor at once after ibn-Saud's departure, the *Quincy* set out for the short run to Alexandria, and much of the following day was given over to a final conference between the President and Mr. Churchill. When the Prime Minister took both of F.D.R.'s hands in his own at parting, neither of the two strong men had any prescience that they were never to see each other again, and talked gaily of meeting soon, either in Washington or London. Vital was the right word for the President as we sailed away from Alexandria for home. At a luncheon given for the correspondents he talked for two hours, going over Yalta high lights; and all agreed that he was never in better form. This is not my own unsupported assertion; for here is the statement of Robert G. Nixon of the International News Service:

On the cruiser crossing the Atlantic on the way home from the Yalta conference, we [the correspondents traveling with the President] had lunch with him in the captain's quarters. The President talked for nearly two hours. His conversation was engaging and covered a vast range of subjects. He spoke movingly when he dwelt upon the plans for making and securing a peace that would save the world from being plunged into another bloody war for generations to come. He was a man whose visions took him centuries into the future. And these thoughts that he expressed were always of how to better the lot of mankind.*

At Algiers, where we stopped to top-off with oil, the President invited De Gaulle to come aboard for luncheon. Evidently the General was still nursing his grievances, for he sent back a somewhat curt refusal. Now setting out on the last lap of our journey, all of us looked forward to seeing Gibraltar by daylight. Steaming through the Straits gave us our first taste of the dangers that lurk in a war zone. Two German submarines were waiting for us outside, but British destroyers intercepted them, and we heard next day that one had been sunk by depth bombs.

In view of the exhausting nature of the Yalta conference, I had counted on the voyage back home to give the President a chance for the rest that he so sorely needed. That hope went glimmering when Sam Rosenman boarded the *Quincy* at Algiers, F.D.R. having summoned him from London where the Judge was on a fact-finding mission. Every morning and part of each afternoon the two worked over the Yalta report. What the President had in mind was not any mere recital of high lights, but a full account, not only to Congress but to the whole people. A drudging business, for after Sam had whipped the dictated matter into shape,

* Copyright, 1945, by International News Service.

F.D.R. went over it word by word, amending and adding so that no detail would be omitted.

On the morning of the twentieth, suddenly and tragically, General Watson passed away. Ailing at Yalta, he suffered a cerebral hemorrhage in Alexandria; but, while his condition was serious, he had shown signs of improvement. What made it harder to bear was that Pa had always been the picture of health, radiating vigor and love of life. The death of his friend came as a terrible shock to the President.

Up to that moment I do not think that the thought of death had ever entered his mind. Aside from natural buoyancy and sanguine temperament, there was his absorption in the job and the immediacy of the tasks that lay before him. Not even the passing of many near and dear associates, as strong and vital as himself, had shaken belief in his own invulnerability. If such were the case now, there was no indication other than his being less communicative in the days following the General's death and his increased activity in the preparation of the reports that he was drawing up for the Congress.

CHAPTER XVIII

THE LOAD TAKES TOLL

A RUSH OF THINGS CAUGHT UP THE PRESIDENT FROM the moment of his return. The forenoon of March 1, the morning after our arrival, saw him drive through the rain and sleet to Arlington, where Pa Watson was buried with appropriate ceremonies. At noon he proceeded to the Capitol for the delivery of his Yalta report. The address, as prepared for official release, contained no reference to his health, but he had been told of the "sick man" stories that were being circulated, and they stirred him to retort. As a result, when he took his chair before the microphones, for we had agreed against standing up, he started off with this extemporaneous interpolation:

I hope you will pardon me for the unusual posture of sitting down during the presentation of what I want to say, but I know you will realize that it makes it a lot easier for me in not having to carry about ten pounds of steel around on the bottom of my legs, and also because I have just completed a 14,000-mile trip. I am returning from this trip, which took me so far, refreshed and inspired. I was well the entire time. I was not ill for a second until I arrived back in Washington. Here I heard all of the rumors which occurred in my absence. Yes, I re- turned from the trip refreshed and inspired—the Roose- velts are not, as you may suspect, averse to travel. We seem to thrive on it.

The New York *Times* reported that he "looked the part as he sat tanned and glowing under a battery of floodlights," but a doctor's more discerning eye could see signs of weariness before the end of the hour re- quired by the length of the address. His voice sagged, and every now and then he passed his hand over his eyes as if to clear his sight. I made this the occasion of a preachment on his return to the White House, but he blamed it on the lights.

After a month's absence, the President's desk was piled high; and, despite my protests, he broke away from his regimen in many vital particulars. Once again the rolling steam table was wheeled to his desk in the executive offices, and every luncheon became a confer- ence. Worse still, he would not take his afternoon rest, skipped his daily rub, and worked far into the night. Checkups continued to be satisfactory, showing no evidence of organic ailment, but each new day added to signs of fatigue. When I remonstrated, he gave the answer to which I was becoming accustomed. "There is a job to be done, and just so much time in which to do it."

A coal strike threatened, and although workers were

leaving war plants in droves, the Congress refused his appeal to enact a man-power bill. The Senate, after grudging confirmation of Henry Wallace as Secretary of Commerce, had rejected Aubrey Williams, one of the President's close friends, as head of the Rural Electrification Commission. Resignations and internal dissension compelled a reshuffling of department heads, a worry and an irritation.

On the other hand, happily, there were some bright spots. His old friend ibn-Saud had declared war on the Axis powers according to promise, and from Russia came word that Stalin would break with Japan. Both in Europe and the Pacific victory now stood assured. With the vaunted West Wall smashed, four Allied armies were on the Rhine for a final thrust, while the Russians battered everything before them on the eastern front. Japan, reeling under hammer blows from sea and air, was being readied for the kill by Nimitz and MacArthur. With the end of fighting in plain sight, it was the peace and its problems that were now his intense preoccupation.

San Francisco, naturally, had first place in the President's thought, and after much deliberation he had decided to go there for the opening of the United Nations rather than the closing. A London visit, begged by Mr. Churchill, was planned for June, and after that he wanted to go deep into the Pacific war zone, even as far as China. Admiral Wilson Brown and I were actually put to work on a travel schedule. By way of preparation, I urged him to go to Warm Springs at once for a real rest, but instead of that he went to Hyde Park for a week end. Not only did it tire him, because of the usual flood of guests; but, worse still, he suffered a gastrointestinal upset that put him completely off his food.

Deeply disturbed, I insisted on a frank talk about his condition, and as we sat face to face, I did not mince words or pull a single punch. As in our discussion at the outset of the 1944 campaign, I repeated my warning that he was no longer a young man able to take liberties with his health. Admitting that tests proved him organically sound, I stressed the dangers of lowered resistance, pointing out that a run-down condition opened the door to every variety of ill.

Since Yalta he had continued to lose weight and was now at least fifteen pounds below normal. If, as planned, he wanted to go to San Francisco and then to London and China, he must regain that poundage and start living within his reserve. Speaking as a doctor to a patient, I told him that it was *mandatory* that he return to the rules of daily living that had kept him fit for twelve years. Not only must he return to them, but it was imperative that he *stay* with them.

The President, considerably impressed, finally quit his contradictions and dissents. Confessing that he had been driving himself too hard, he gave his solemn promise that he would be a good patient, neither playing hooky nor running out on a single rule. A month in Warm Springs was decided on, and after seeing him safely installed, I left his care in the capable hands of Commander Bruenn and Commander George Fox, the physiotherapist who had tended him since 1933.

His heart, quite naturally, was our principal concern. Why not? Here was a man of sixty-three, under terrific strain for years, who had been coughing heavily for more than two months in the spring of 1944. Time proved that our fears were groundless, for that stout heart of his never failed, but we could not foresee that this would be the case. As for cerebral hemorrhage, it was and is unpredictable. There are some conditions, of course, in which we think we can predict it, such as extremely high blood pressure and advanced general arteriolosclerosis although there is no certainty.

President Roosevelt did not have either of these. His blood pressure was not alarming at any time; in fact, on the morning of the day he died, it was well within normal limits for a man of his age. I have talked to many excellent pathologists and have yet to find one willing to say that he can tell when a man will have a cerebral hemorrhage or when he will not. The signs that we count on for the condition of the cerebral arteries all denied that the President would have any trouble in that regard. His kidneys and liver functions were normal.

From the first the daily reports were most encouraging. Daisy, the colored cook, toiled happily in the preparation of dishes that would tempt the President's appetite, and he was putting on weight. Best of all, perfect weather permitted long drives, and these hours in the sun gave him a fine coat of tan. Keeping strictly to the letter of our agreement, he had received only two callers—Henry Morgenthau and Sergio Osmena, President of the Philippines. The Osmena visit was more of a celebration than anything else, for the islands had been freed, and the President joyously outlined a broad program of reconstruction to repair the ravages of war.

When Dr. Bruenn telephoned on Thursday, April 12, his report was most optimistic. The President had gained back eight of his lost pounds and was feeling so fit that he planned to attend an old-fashioned Georgia barbecue in the afternoon and a minstrel show that evening for the Foundation's patients. Every cause for anxiety seemed to have lifted, and given another lazy, restful week, there was no reason why he should not return to Washington on April 20 to greet the Regent of Iraq.

After asking Dr. Bruenn to tell the President that I would be down for the week end, I decided to take Dr. James Paullin with me. In view of the proposed trip to San Francisco, with London and China to follow in all probability, a thorough checkup appeared to be advisable, even if not indicated as necessary. Telephoning Atlanta, I made my arrangement with Dr. Paullin and had just hung up when Dr. Bruenn called back. The President, he said, had fainted, and was still unconscious.

This had happened at twenty minutes after one, just as luncheon was about to be served and while he was chatting gaily with his cousins, Miss Suckley and Miss Delano, Bill Hassett, and Mrs. Elizabeth Shoumatoff, the artist who was painting his portrait. All commented afterward on his "high spirits" and "how well he looked." Suddenly, and while a laugh was on his lips, he complained of a terrible headache, and collapsed in his chair.

Dr. Bruenn went on to tell me that he had rushed in to find the President pale, cold, sweating profusely, and totally unconscious. Making no effort to conceal his alarm, he reported that the pupils of the eyes were equal at first, but that the left had become widely dilated in a few seconds. Paralysis was also present. Stating that he had instituted emergency measures to relieve the intense vasostriction, Bruenn ended by saying he would make another report in five minutes.

Getting Dr. Paullin again, I asked him to race at once to Warm Springs, and learned later that he had made the eighty miles in a little more than an hour. This done, I rang Steve Early, asking him to get in touch with Mrs. Roosevelt, and then ordered a Navy plane to stand by. Dr. Bruenn, on his second call, confirmed my fears, giving it as his opinion that the President had suffered a cerebral hemorrhage. Nevertheless, he held out hope, for the heart rate was excellent, the breathing good, the color improved, and the blood pressure showed signs of falling. He was continuing to use aminophyllin, nitroglycerin, and other remedies.

Telephoning a third time, some minutes later, Dr. Bruenn said that Dr. Paullin had arrived and was at the bedside. Before he had fairly started to give me details, however, I heard him utter a startled exclamation, and the sudden silence made me know that he had been summoned back into the sickroom. It seemed ages that I waited, but it could only have been a matter of seconds when someone else picked up the telephone, and a broken, tear-choked voice informed me that the President was no more.

Dr. Paullin's report, sent subsequently, gave these details of the last moments:

The President was *in extremis* when I reached him. He was in a cold sweat, ashy gray, and breathing with difficulty. Numerous rhonchi in his chest. He was propped up in bed. His pupils were dilated, and his hands slightly cyanosed. Commander Bruenn had started artificial respiration. On examination his pulse was barely perceptible. His heart sounds could be heard, but about three and a half minutes after my arrival, they disappeared completely. I gave him an intracardiac dose of adrenalin in the hope that we might stimulate his heart to action. However, his lungs were full of rales, both fine, medium and coarse, and his blood pressure was not obtainable. There were no effects from the adrenalin except perhaps for two or three beats of the heart, which did not continue. Within five minutes after my entrance into the

242

room, all evidence of life had passed away. The time was 3:35 o'clock.

Mrs. Roosevelt, Steve Early, and I, hurrying to the plane, reached Warm Springs at eleven that night. In the discussion that followed our arrival, an autopsy was decided against as there was no useful purpose to be served by it. Both Dr. Paullin and Commander Bruenn were in agreement that the cause of death was a "massive intracerebral hemorrhage which, in all probability, had ruptured into the subarachnoid space."

There was no confusion or debate as to the funeral arrangements; for the President, long before, had selected the lawn in the rose garden at Hyde Park as the spot where he wished to take the last rest. The train bearing his body rolled north through a lane of mourning men, women, and little children, and under the sun of a Sabbath morning the fallen warrior returned to the home that he loved.

For those close to him, it will always be a bitter regret that Franklin Roosevelt could not have lived to share in the triumph that was so largely the result of his force and vision; that he could not have continued to pour the flame of his faith into the world organization that was the highest hope in a heart that had no room for any but high hopes. Yet not one of those who knew him best and loved him the most believes that he would have voiced a protest or filed any claim of unfairness. The *will to serve* had carried him

243

through killing labors, victorious over every weakness of the body until the job had been done. And with him, it was only the job that ever counted. And in his last words, "The only limit to our realization of tomorrow will be our doubts of today. Let us move forward with strong and active faith."